# THE HANDICRAFTS OF FRANCE

AS RECORDED IN THE

*Descriptions des Arts et Métiers*

Henri-Louis Duhamel du Monceau, the scholar who brought the *Descriptions*
to fruition.

# THE HANDICRAFTS OF FRANCE

AS RECORDED IN THE

*Descriptions des Arts et Métiers* 1761-1788

BY

ARTHUR H. COLE

*Librarian, Baker Library*

AND

GEORGE B. WATTS

*Professor of French, Davidson College*

BAKER LIBRARY

HARVARD GRADUATE SCHOOL OF BUSINESS ADMINISTRATION

SOLDIERS FIELD, BOSTON, MASSACHUSETTS

Publication Number 8 of

The Kress Library of Business and Economics

This undertaking was made possible in part through a grant-in-aid to Professor Watts allocated by a research committee at Davidson College, from funds made available jointly by the Carnegie Foundation and that College. The authors, however, and not the College or the Foundation, are wholly responsible for the statements made in this monograph.

PRINTED AT THE
HARVARD UNIVERSITY PRINTING OFFICE
CAMBRIDGE, MASSACHUSETTS, U. S. A.

# DESCRIPTIONS DES ARTS ET MÉTIERS

DIDEROT is credited with the statement that if the peoples of early times had compounded an encyclopedia and if this document alone had escaped the destruction of the Alexandrine Library, it would have consoled us for the loss of all else in that institution. While one could easily find bases for argument against such a proposition, there is an element of importance in this assertion in so far as an encyclopedia summarizes the state of knowledge existent at the time of its formulation. The subject of this brochure — the *Descriptions des Arts et Métiers*, published by the Académie Royale des Sciences of Paris in 1761–1788 — aimed to be encyclopedic in nature (though not so in form): it constituted an effort to present a scientific picture of all the industrial processes employed in France in the eighteenth century. Since no corresponding survey was carried through in any other country at so early a date and since this one in France anticipated but briefly the industrial changes commonly associated with the phrase, "the industrial revolution," these volumes are worthy of particular notice. In a sense, they portray the maxima of skills attained at the end of a social period, the age of the handicraftsman. Moreover, there can be no doubt that contemporaneously these descriptions of arts and handicrafts created a wide interest and exerted a potent influence in western Europe — although the greater renown of Diderot's *Encyclopédie*, which was appearing during much of the same period (1751–1780), the French Revolution, and the development of many new techniques in the latter eighteenth and in the nineteenth centuries have pushed this rather extraordinary effort into an oblivion which it does not deserve.[1]

Likewise there are some aspects of this series — an outstanding example of the high plane attained by the French printers, engravers, and publishers of the times — which are of significance for the librarian and the bibliographer. Brunet in his *Manuel du libraire* does not give a wholly accurate list of the items that compose this group of industrial surveys, whereas Graesse does little other than to copy Brunet's statement, with errors. Lanson in his *Manuel bibliographique* fails to mention the *Descriptions* and the majority of its authors, and biographies such as *La France littéraire*, the *Nouvelle Biographie Générale*, and the *Biographie Universelle* treat this collection and its collab-

---

[1] Typical of more recent comments is that of Brunet who, in listing the several units of this series in the fifth edition of his *Manuel*, states that scarcely forty years earlier the collection formed a necessary part of all the great libraries and sold for five to six hundred francs when it was complete — which state was difficult to find — but the progress of mechanical and industrial arts had rendered the greater part of these descriptions almost useless, and that he reproduces the list of individual volumes only because they might still interest some people. (Brunet, Jacques Charles, *Manuel du libraire*, 5th ed., Paris, 1860, v. 2, p. 620). Graesse in his *Trésor de livres rares et précieux* (Dresden, 1859–69) gives an equally unfavorable comment (v. 2, p. 366).

orators inadequately, whereas the printed catalogue of the Bibliothèque Nationale fails repeatedly to identify particular volumes as parts of this set.
Again, it is noteworthy that many American libraries have not seen the importance of analyzing this series of monographs, although often nowhere else can
one find any description at all of certain arts and handicrafts of the eighteenth
century — here always illustrated with drawings of tools and workshops —
and more frequently still no descriptions that rival in completeness of detail
those which form parts of this group of individual units.[2]

## The Nature of the Descriptions

The title which the Academy selected for the series is highly appropriate.
The volumes are descriptions of the arts and handicrafts and hardly anything
else. Typically, a monograph consists of a section explaining the several varie-
ties of raw materials employed, a section describing the tools and other equipment utilized, and a third section portraying in detail the steps which the
workmen must carry through in turning out the several products, to which

[2] There are two known full sets and seven known sets of varying degrees of completeness in
American libraries. The American Philosophical Society of Philadelphia has a twenty-four volume
set, with few omissions. There is no record of the source of this collection. The Boston Athenaeum
Library has on permanent deposit the set in thirty-two volumes, willed by Dr. Franklin to the
American Academy of Arts and Sciences of Boston. This collection was housed in the Athenaeum
from 1817 until 1899, when it was moved to the Academy's library on Newbury Street. In 1947
the Franklin set was returned to the Athenaeum. According to the report for the year 1947, "it is
hoped that it may be possible in the near future to build a suitable exhibition case for these books
in the Newspaper Reading Room, so that they may be shown in the room that the Academy occu-
pied for half a century." The Baker Library of the Harvard Graduate School of Business Administration has in the Kress Library a set in fifty-three volumes, bound in modern leather. Several
of the arts are bound separately. There are certain duplications and omissions. The Davidson
College Library has an incomplete set in twenty-seven volumes, bound in calf. This was once the
property of Sanlot de Bospin, an *Administrateur Général des Domaines et Droits Domaniaux* from
1781 until the Revolution. The Harvard College Library has a set in eighteen volumes, bound in
calf, complete through 1779. This set, now safely housed in the Houghton Library, carries the
added interest of being the gift to Harvard by John Adams, "Vice-President of the United States."
It was recorded on June 5, 1789. The Metropolitan Museum of Art has a complete set in thirty-
three volumes, purchased from the income of the Jacob S. Rogers Fund. The New York Public
Library has a set, bound in boards, a part of an originally complete collection in fifty-three volumes, eighteen of which are missing. The Stanford University Library has an incomplete set in
thirty-four volumes, through 1777, given to it by Timothy Hopkins, a close friend of the Stanford
family and a life member of the board of trustees of the university. The United States Patent
Office has the second known full set in the United States. It is in forty-five volumes, cloth sides
with leather backs, catalogued in October, 1856. It has, in addition to all the cahiers of the original
edition, the three descriptions which are sometimes listed as making up a part of the collection.
(See Appendix A, Addendum.)

American libraries which have known portions of the original edition are: Boston Public Library (10); Cleveland Public Library (1); Library of Congress (11); Lehigh University Library
(1); Massachusetts Institute of Technology Library (1); University of Michigan Library (11);
University of Pennsylvania Library (7); Princeton University Library (1); Western Reserve University Library (1); Yale University Library (3); Yale School of Music Library (1); Library
Company of Philadelphia (7), Library of Engineering Societies of New York (1).

The Neufchâtel edition of the series exists in the Boston Athenaeum, the University of California Library, the Grosvenor Library of Buffalo, the Library Company of Philadelphia (this set
was willed to it by Dr. Franklin. Volume 19 is missing), and the United States Patent Office.
Among American libraries owning separate titles of this edition are: Boston Public Library (1);
Harvard College Library (1); and the New York Public Library (1).

is added a series of engravings that picture both the tools and the workshops. Every effort is made to render the descriptions realistic and practical: the explanations of processes are tied in with the picturizations of equipment, and the drawings of the shops exhibit the workmen at their benches or otherwise carrying out the various operations. Sometimes, to be sure, a section is introduced covering the trade in raw materials; occasionally there is a reference to the market for the finished commodities; and in some cases there are brief histories of the particular arts, and appendices defining the terms used in the handicrafts. (A typical engraving, concerned in this case with the art of playing card production, is reproduced herewith.) On the other hand, no effort is made to portray the economic significance of the several industries with which the various handicrafts are associated, to indicate the size of the establishments, or to present data upon government policies toward the several manufactures.

The participants in the venture included a number of distinguished figures in eighteenth century France. Of the two most active and influential contributors, MM. de Réaumur and Duhamel du Monceau, a good bit will be said in a later connection. Among the others one could cite Gabriel Jars, known for his *Voyages métallurgiques*, the distinguished astronomers, Joseph-Jérôme Le Français de Lalande and Pierre-Charles Le Monnier, the mathematician Charles Romme, the chemist Paul-Jacques Malouin, one of the original group of "Encyclopédistes," the physician Jean-François-Clément Morand, and Roland de la Platière, a minister of the interior in the early days of the French Revolution and husband of the celebrated Madame Roland. Moreover, the Academy did not hesitate to draw upon foreign talent when appropriate material from their pens was available. Two Swedish writers were thus honored. Fredrik Henrik Chapman's *Treatise on ship-building*, which had appeared in Stockholm in 1775, was translated and printed in full; while substantial excerpts were translated from Emmanuel Swedenborg's *Treatise on iron* (originally written in Latin and published in Dresden and Leipzig in 1734).[2a]

The arts and handicrafts comprehended in these several volumes cover a large part of French industrial activity of that period — as is indicated by the list of individual volumes, presented with full bibliographical detail below (Appendix A) — and in some degree the economic importance of the several crafts is reflected in the amount of space devoted to their respective descriptions. Thus there are substantial studies of coal mining and organ making; there are a number of items concerned with metal working; some 1,300 pages and nearly 400 plates are devoted to carpentry; a half dozen units relate to the textiles; while less extensive explanations are presented of the making of hats, the manufacture of soap, the production of candles, and the art of the

[2a] Brief biographical sketches of the various contributors are presented in Appendix C.

barber.[3] Only in a minor degree is the general thread of the series broken: the description of arts and handicrafts. One brief monograph does describe a new variety of microscope; another discusses a new method for scaling mathematical and astronomical instruments; and prior to his explanation of the method of painting upon glass, M. Le Vieil gives a lengthy history of that art; Dom Bedos de Celles likewise presents, in the preface to the fourth and last part of his famous treatise, a history of the organ; while Duhamel du Monceau's extensive *General treatise on fishes*, which, although an integral part of the series, was often sold separately and is not listed in the last catalogue of the publisher, does include a great deal of zoology as well as a description of fishing techniques. On the whole, however, one could not refuse a decision that the Academy of Sciences had by 1788 accomplished the aim which it had set before itself in the early days of the century. The progress, especially from the inception of the plan to the beginning of publication, had been slow, but the goal had been reached. Moreover, the total publication — all in folio dimensions — had grown to aggregate a small library in itself. It attained almost 13,500 pages of text and the volumes contained over 1,800 plates.[4]

## ORIGIN OF THE SERIES

The *Descriptions des arts et métiers* derives in a sense from the activities of that great French economic statesman, Jean-Baptiste Colbert. In 1666 the latter gave organization and prestige to an informal group of scholars, among whom were Descartes, Gassendi, and Blaise and Étienne Pascal, which, since the early part of the seventeenth century, had been meeting in private homes.

[3] In further evidence upon this point, it may be noted that the "art" of making tennis rackets is confined to thirty-four textual pages and five plates, but the "art" of manufacturing silk cloth is divided into seven sections, runs to nearly 1,500 pages of description, and includes 177 engravings. Similarly, the manufacture of pins is covered in seventy-seven pages and seven plates, while the study of coal mining requires 1,656 pages and nearly seventy illustrations.

[4] It is a little difficult to state just how many items the whole series constituted. One would have to be somewhat arbitrary in defining the term "item." In the list presented in Appendix A, eighty-one separate entries may be counted, if supplements or corrections — usually by variant authors and often separately issued — are considered independent units, and only seventy-three entries, if these additive items are not so counted. The term "volume" is yet more meaningless. Several of the smaller items are usually bound togther, whereas the combined studies on iron working by Courtivron and others or Duhamel du Monceau's treatise on fish must be bound into several separate units or volumes. As has been seen above (note to p. 2) there is a wide variety in the number of volumes in the several sets consulted in American libraries. The problem of what constituted a "volume" apparently plagued eighteenth century readers and binders, for in the last catalogue — printed by Moutard in 1783 with Lucotte's *L'art de la maçonnerie* — there is a suggested order "which one may observe in binding the collection of *Arts et Métiers*, and which is the same as the one used for the set of the Royal Academy of Sciences." After indicating fourteen possible "volumes," the printer, perhaps with a sense of frustration, says: "The others are not numerous enough on the same matter to be bound together." Further evidence of this difficulty is seen in the suggestion accompanying the last part of *L'art du facteur d'orgues*, where the printer states: "It was made to be bound in a single volume to which one will assign the following arrangement: after the title page one will put the preface, then the table of chapters and sections, then the corrections and additions, then the first, second, third, and fourth parts, the table of contents, and the plates." A similar suggestion was found necessary by the printer of Morand's *L'art d'exploiter les mines de charbon de terre*. Small wonder that the director of an American library, confronted with the task of cataloguing his set, said: "It looks like a mare's nest to me."

He established the Royal Academy of Sciences, gave it a meeting place in the library of the king, and looked with favor upon its activities. Louis XIV himself — probably under Colbert's influence — set up pensions for some of the distinguished scholars and provided funds for the annual expenses of experiments.[5]

The Academy was composed at this time chiefly of mathematicians and physicists, and little attention seems to have been given in the early years or even in the first decades of the Academy's existence to problems of the applied sciences. To be sure, the general idea of a wholesale delineation of French manufacturing techniques was put forward at the very beginning of the life of the Academy. In 1666, each academician was invited to outline his own program of future Academy activities. Thereupon, Auzout, an astronomer, is reported to have asked that some members of the group should be commissioned to inspect French workmen, their tools and their instruments, the manner in which the latter were used, to discover what the workmen needed (presumably for improvement in their operations), and to apprehend their secrets and their "sophistications."[6] In pursuit of this suggestion, another academician, Couplet, was charged with carrying forward this idea. But nothing immediately seems to have derived from the proposal, except perhaps the introduction of some greater attention to mechanical inventions than might otherwise have concerned the group. The history of the Academy compounded at the beginning of the eighteenth century presents a section in the annual account of Academy proceedings which it entitles "Mécaniques." The first entry of this type relates to the year 1668; and for most of the years thereafter (through the rest of the century) there is some mention of developments in the field of mechanics. The entries are short, however, seem often to be concerned with physics, and surely have nothing in common with M. Auzout's program.

Colbert appears to have stuck in his oar more positively a decade after the Academy had been launched. In the report of the above-mentioned history for 1675, there is an illuminating statement:

The king wished the Academy to work unceasingly upon a treatise on mechanics, in which theory and practice should be applied with clarity and in a manner within everyone's

[5] The antecedents of the Royal Academy of Sciences are carefully elaborated in Harcourt Brown's *Scientific organizations in seventeenth century France* (Baltimore, 1934). In this history it becomes apparent that the development of scientific bodies was not continuous and unilinear, and that an important immediate influence on French governmental policy was the establishment of the Royal Society in London in 1660.

[6] Evidence in Brown's volume, just cited, shows that Auzout was quite surely not the originator of the idea but a transmitter of early thought. The Montmor "academy" in a constitution of 1657 had stated as one of its chief objectives "the improvement of the conveniences of life, in the arts and sciences which seek to establish them" (Brown, p. 75), while a *Projet* of 1663 or 1664, drawn up in outlining the desired Royal Academy, was even more specific: invention of new machines to be encouraged, improvements of old ones to be sought actively, and practices of artisans in France and elsewhere to be learned and recorded (*ibid.*, p. 146). Auzout was both a member of the Montmor group and a person active in the promotion of the Academy.

understanding. . . In this treatise should be described all the machines then utilized in the practice of the handicrafts in France or in foreign countries.

This was what M. Colbert made known to the Academy through M. Perrault on the nineteenth of June in this year. The Academy devoted several of its meetings to consideration of this subject; and M. Du Hamel (the secretary) was instructed to report to M. Colbert the consensus of the written opinions of the members. . .

M. Buot commenced at once to describe some of the manufacturing equipment most commonly in use or at least where the use is best known. . .

Yet this intervention of the powerful Colbert brought no significant results, at least in the years that came immediately after, even though this "directive" of 1675 was followed closely — in 1681 — by a visit of the king to the Academy, a visit which we may imagine was engineered by the economic statesman. Nor was Colbert's successor, Louvois, any more successful. As early as 1686, he indicated an interest in the Academy and endeavored, in fact, to direct its attention at least in part to studies which would "have importance for the service of the State." [7]

Perhaps the times were not yet ripe. Perhaps this endeavor suffered as did all the other activities of the Academy from the revocation of the Edict of Nantes which exiled two of the Academy's most distinguished members, Huyghens and Romme. At all events, the institution appears to have undergone a serious decline in the last decades of the seventeenth century. Absence of members from its meetings seems to have increased; the laboratory was abandoned; and the promising start of 1666 appeared in danger of yielding no permanent fruit.

Revival of the Academy and renewal of the scheme for describing French handicrafts had to await the active intervention of the potent Abbé Bignon. By virtue of the latter's influence, the institution experienced a second birth in 1699; a constitution was elaborated, and was promulgated by the king; enlarged financial support was extended to the Academy and to its new hierarchy of students, associates, and pensionnaires; and under these favorable circumstances, the body revived and flourished.

In some measure, the constitution or charter of the Academy carried forward the notion that earlier had been expressed by Auzout, Colbert, and Louvois. Among the pensionnaires, numbering twenty in all, at least three were to be "mécaniciens"; and of the associates, two were to be men "appliquez aux mécaniques." The academicians were urged (by Article 22 of the Règlement) to extend their researches to all that might be of use or interest in the variant conduct of the handicrafts. Moreover, the Academy was given a practical administrative task in the area of applied science, namely, the examination of all the machines for which patents were sought from the king. It was

[7] Louvois' admonitions to the Academy were probably not well received; to this body of scientists who were apparently endeavoring to work with all seriousness, he proposed that they distinguish between research "which was only pure curiosity or which could only be described as the amusement of the chemists" from that which would have consequence for the nation!

to certify whether the machines were new and useful; and the inventors of approved devices were to leave models with the Academy.

Now for the first time the Academy appears to have outlined for itself the program which later came to fruition in the *Descriptions des arts et métiers*. Regarding the year 1699, the *Histoire* of the Academy contains a rather elaborate statement respecting this scheme — a statement which is translated quite literally:

The work of invention is the pleasantest and at the same time the sort most likely to gain glory, and one would naturally be quite carried away in pursuing it to the exclusion of all others. But, since the Academy has in mind really to be of service to the public rather than to please itself or to win public esteem, it has voluntarily embraced a task which is dry, thorny, and not at all showy, that of describing the crafts in their present condition in France.

This description will penetrate to the minutest details, although there may be great difficulties either in gathering the facts from the workmen or in explaining them; and it will present by text or by illustrations all the raw materials, tools, and operations employed by the handicraftsman.

By this means, an infinity of practical methods, full of skill and inventiveness, but unknown to the general public, will be drawn out from the shadows.

Posterity can thus be assured of the crafts, at least as they exist among us now. It will always be able to rediscover them by turning to this collection, in spite of revolutions; and if we have lost some of those that were important to our forebears, it is because use was not made of a similar means for transmitting them to us.

Men who cannot take the trouble or lack the leisure to go to study the crafts at the shops of the workmen will be able to see them here almost at a glance — if they are men of any ability — and will be induced by this means to work toward perfecting them. The Academy will not fail to note where, in its judgment, something might be added or might, at least, be desirable.

When this work is completed, it will be easy for each craft to compare the practices in vogue in France with those pursued in other countries; and from this comparison, the French and the inhabitants of these foreign lands will profit equally.

No evidence has survived as to who, in fact, was the author of this outline or statement of objectives. One is inclined to suspect the aforesaid Abbé Bignon [8] but conceivably it could have been one M. des Billettes, who began almost immediately after 1699 to report to the Academy on various matters closely akin to this program. Yet, whoever was the source of this inspiration, there is no doubt that the scheme of describing French arts and handicrafts had definitely been launched.

The new turn of Academy interest was evident almost immediately. M. Jaugeon, with the later collaboration of M. des Billettes and Père Sebastien Truchet, prepared, beginning even in 1699, a description of that "art which was to preserve all the others, the art of writing and printing." [9] M. des

[8] One additional bit of evidence favoring the Abbé is the statement in the *Histoire* for 1702 that he "had charged" one Louis Carré to describe all musical instruments as a means of hastening "the general enterprise of the description of the arts."

[9] The manuscript of this treatise — which is entitled *Description et perfection des arts et métiers: Des arts de construire les caractères, de graver les poinçons des lettres, de fondre les lettres, d'imprimer les lettres et de relier les livres:* Tome premier, par M. Jaugeon, de l'Académie royale

Billettes reported in 1700 on the making of pins and in 1703 on the art of copper-plate engraving. In the same year M. Jaugeon gave a paper on the stamping of dies. In fact, these two gentlemen submitted before 1710 more than a dozen memoirs dealing with industrial subjects. From 1711 to 1725 M. de Réaumur prepared at least seven papers on such diversified subjects as the fabrication of artificial pearls, mirror making, and iron mines. With the participation in the effort by M. de Réaumur, the first real editor or entrepreneur of the series comes into view. According to the eulogy that was compounded at his death, it appears that he was, as early as 1706, charged with the whole program outlined in 1699, and that thereafter he devoted himself largely to that project.

M. de Réaumur is one of three figures whose names are particularly associated with the development of the *Descriptions*. The first is the shadowy individual, probably the Abbé Bignon, who sponsored and outlined the plan in the last year of the seventeenth century. The second was Réaumur, who, according to his biographer, came to the attention of the Academy as in some measure a protégé of the good Abbé.

This extraordinary Frenchman deserves more than passing attention. He was one of those whom Professor Nef doubtless had in mind in pointing out the beneficent conditions of the eighteenth century in France for advance in scientific and technical knowledge: the considerable political stability, the faith in the rational powers of the mind, the high moral standards, and the love of beauty, which together provided "the leisure and the calm essential to the best work . . . in the service of science." [10]

Born in 1683 of well-to-do parents, he studied with the Jesuits at Poitiers — displaying already an inclination to mathematics and physics — and, at the early age of twenty, took himself to Paris. In the next five years he had displayed such notable talents that he was elected a member of the Academy and at once began the presentation, as seen above, of a series of memoirs, which, in fact, extended pretty well through his lifetime.[11]

Remembered today only for his elaboration of a new type of thermometer, his influence during his life was great both in the field of applied science and in that of the natural sciences. His researches resulted in the establishment of new manufactures and the revival of neglected industries. In the area of applied science his most important publication was his *L'art de convertir le fer forgé en acier et l'art d'adoucir le fer fondu*, issued in 1722. In this volume, based on a long series of experiments, Réaumur brought to the knowledge of

des sciences (1704, in- fol., 424 p., with drawings and engraved plates) — is preserved in the library of the Institute. The same library has a collection of pen sketches, wash drawings, and engravings, dated 1693, 1703, 1712, and 1717, which had been prepared for the proposed series.

[10] Nef, John U., "The industrial revolution reconsidered," *Journal of economic history*, v. 3 (1943), p. 27.

[11] A somewhat popular study of his career is to be found in Jean Torlais' *Un esprit encyclopédique en dehors de "L'encyclopédie": Réaumur* (Paris, 1936).

French metallurgists the cementation process of steel production (which had already been developed in England), and sought to demonstrate its applicability to the iron ores of France. Historians of the French iron and steel industry are not unanimous in their belief that his findings were really suitable to French conditions in the degree to which he believed them; but even a hostile critic of the mid-nineteenth century speaks of Réaumur's "celebrated experiments of 1715–1722," of the "great influence" of his book upon contemporary opinion, and even of the "authority" which his writings exercised as late as the 1840's.[12] Likewise Swank, writing at the close of the nineteenth century, quotes other authorities relative to Réaumur's "celebrated treatise" of 1722.[13] Indicative of the high esteem in which his volume was held in foreign countries is the fact that it was soon translated into German and English. Even today the method of tinning iron which he devised is still employed.

Regarding Réaumur's activities in the field of natural sciences, it is hardly appropriate here to make extended comment. It is perhaps sufficient to speak again of his contribution of a new thermometer and to mention his most extensive publication, the six volume work entitled *Mémoires pour servir à l'histoire des insectes*. Even in the area of natural science his mind had a practical turn, and one of his books which — being translated into both English and German — increased his international fame was his *Art of hatching and bringing up domestick fowls by means of artificial heat* (to use the English form).

A great deal of Réaumur's labors connected with the *Descriptions des arts et métiers* counted for little in his lifetime or at least during his active years. His seemed to have been the work of assembling materials and preparing the ground.[14] When at last in 1761 the first volume of the series was published, the "avertissement général" carried a tribute to him: "M. de Réaumur had been charged with gathering together a substantial number of memoirs which had already been prepared by various academicians as well as others sent from different provinces of France or from foreign countries. These memoirs upon the arts have multiplied. A great number of work-shops, operations, machines, instruments, and tools have been drawn and engraved in the same format; and the Academy now possesses more than 200 plates appropriate to the description of these arts and handicrafts." Undoubtedly much of this accumulation

---

[12] LePlay, M. F., *Mémoire sur la fabrication et le commerce des fers* . . . (Paris, 1846), p. 95.
[13] Swank, James M., *History of the manufacture of iron in all ages*, 2nd ed. (Philadelphia, 1892), p. 97.
[14] If one could take literally a statement by Condorcet in his eulogy before the Academy of Fougeroux de Bondaroy in 1789, it would seem that Réaumur and Duhamel were jointly responsible for the idea of the *Descriptions*. Condorcet says: "It was in the partnership of Réaumur and Duhamel that the plan for the collection of the arts and handicrafts was formulated." This assertion can hardly be accepted, for, without any doubt, the plan of the publication had been born in the early days of the reconstitution of the Academy in 1699, and as early as 1706 the term, *description des arts et métiers*, appears in the *Histoire* of the Academy. It is possible, however, that the actual steps to launch the publication of the *Descriptions* may have been the combined effort of Réaumur and Duhamel.

was due to the zeal of Réaumur. The work had had the support of the regent, the Duke of Orleans, who had provided for the preparation of a "considerable number" of the drawings, many of which had been lost before publication began in 1761. Frequently at the beginning of individual volumes of the *Descriptions*, the author acknowledges his debt to Réaumur and speaks of finding one or several engravings already prepared on his topic in the "dépôt" of the Academy.

M. de Réaumur had inherited means that enabled him to devote himself to research. He was granted a pension of 12,000 livres by the king for his distinguished work in the study of steel technology — a sum which, to be sure, he was allowed to have allocated to the expenses of his work at the Academy; he never married; and he appears to have lived in "the leisure and the calm" which Professor Nef believes to be so important for scientific work.

### THE SECOND STEP: DUHAMEL DU MONCEAU

The death of Réaumur in 1757 made necessary a fresh start. Just how this revival and reorientation was achieved is not evident from the existing record. It is not impossible that the members of the Academy, noting the interest aroused by the first volumes of the *Encyclopédie, ou Dictionnaire raisonné des Sciences, des Arts et des Métiers, etc.*, by Diderot and d'Alembert, and, fearing lest the considerable amount of text and engravings in their "dépôt" might be rendered unusable by the previous publication of similar materials in the *Encyclopédie*, felt a sense of urgency in getting their long projected series into production. At all events, the most circumstantial account of the revival states that on July 15, 1757, the papers that had been found at M. de Réaumur's home — then just recently put in order — were distributed to twenty members of the Academy. These academicians were charged to examine the manuscripts and to publish those that were in condition for immediate appearance; then they were to make additions to the volumes which were incomplete, because of the fact that the arts therein treated had "meanwhile been perfected," to revise materials which were not in appropriate form, and, lastly, to undertake new research relative to the handicrafts which were found not to be covered by Réaumur's papers or others in the possession of the Academy.[15]

No director of the project was designated and apparently no board of editors set up; nor is there any means of identifying surely the twenty academicians to whom the tasks and papers were distributed except on a basis of the authorship of volumes that appeared early in the published series.

Indirect evidence points to Henri Duhamel du Monceau as the principal driving force. Surely his was the first unit in the sequence that appeared, the *Art du charbonnier*, which was published in 1761. Probably, too, he wrote the "avertissement général" — already quoted — that serves both as preface

[15] Lalande, Joseph-Jérôme Le Français de, *Art du tanneur* (1764), pp. vi–viii.

to this volume and as announcement of the intentions and hopes of the Academy for the whole group of prospective volumes.[16] Surely also M. Duhamel du Monceau contributed numerically the greatest quantity of individual studies, a total of twenty, from the *Art du charbonnier* to the *Traité général des pêches*, of which the final part did not appear until the year of the author's death in 1782.

As in the case of M. de Réaumur, it seems worth while to pause a minute to characterize Duhamel du Monceau with some degree of adequacy. In a measure, the two men were much alike. M. Duhamel du Monceau also was born into a family of substantial means; he early indicated an interest in scientific study; he never married; and he was the recipient of royal favor in the provision of an annual honorarium, although as inspector general of the department of the Navy he seems to have been fairly active in the duties of that office. For the most part, however, he was able — as was Réaumur — to devote his life to research in scientific fields.

Duhamel's career differs from that of his illustrious predecessor in so far as apparent rapidity of development is concerned. Although Réaumur had gained access to the Academy by his early twenties and had published his main work on steel-making when he was but thirty-three, Duhamel du Monceau had been admitted to the Academy when he was twenty-eight, but he had published nothing before he was fifty-eight. He had, to be sure, been studying, had been conducting experiments in agricultural techniques for many years, had won his admission to the Academy for his report on his discovery of the fungus which was destroying the saffron plant in Gâtinais, and had begun in 1740 to report to the Academy meteorological observations made at his home in the country. Again, Duhamel du Monceau seems never to have had the interest in mathematics and pure science that Réaumur evinced in his early days and to which he returned occasionally in later years. Duhamel du Monceau was practical. Of the sixty papers which he submitted to the Academy, nearly all are in applied chemistry or botany or mechanics, from a memoir on salt (1737) to one on the iron forges of Brittany (1780).

While he threw himself into the partially done job of preparing and publishing the *Descriptions des arts et métiers*, he quite evidently undertook portions of the work for which he had little or no preparation and perhaps only a scholar's interest — as appears in the prefaces or in footnotes attached to some of the *Descriptions* which he compounded. Moreover, Condorcet in the eulogy which he prepared upon Duhamel's life when the latter died in 1782 quite properly suggested that his subject's name would be found ranked with that change of purpose or, as Condorcet put it, "revolution" among men of genius which directed the sciences more particularly to public service; and

[16] On pp. 1611–1612 of Morand's *L'art d'exploiter les mines de charbon de terre* it is said that this *avertissement* had been published in 1759 and had "been inserted at the head of the description of the art of the coal-miner."

not without a good deal of propriety he added that no one had contributed more than Duhamel du Monceau to that change.[17]

The scientific interests of Duhamel were broad. While he was concerned with his descriptions of the handicrafts of candle-making and the refining of sugar or those of the locksmith, the slater, and the maker of playing cards, and although we are likely to be impressed by the extensive treatise on fishes and commercial fishing which forms a part of the *Descriptions*, his fame rests perhaps more largely upon his studies in agriculture and the allied field of forestry. Surely that was the work most widely recognized in his lifetime. His *Practical treatise on husbandry* and his *Elements of agriculture* were translated into English as well as into German and Spanish; and the great exponent of improvement in British agriculture, the celebrated Arthur Young, made a special detour in his journeys through France of 1787–89, as he put it, to view "the seat of the late celebrated Mons. du Hamel . . . where he made those experiments in agriculture which he has recited in many of his works . . . I walked thither for the pleasure of viewing the grounds I had read of so often, considering them with a sort of classic reverence." [18]

Nor has Duhamel du Monceau's stature grown less with the years. In a recent reassessment of eighteenth-century agricultural improvement in England and particularly of the work of that notable innovator, Jethro Tull, it is stated that "Tull, forgotten by his countrymen, has been remembered by the French. M. Duhamel du Monceau, a distinguished savant . . . had been impressed by Tull's book (of which he had seen an incomplete translation) and had been stimulated by it to pursue a line of research (which ultimately came to publication) under the title, *Traité de la culture des terres suivant les principes de M. Tull*. This title was generous, for the work was mainly original . . . Duhamel did not swallow Tull whole, much he rejected and was wise enough to say so, with emphasis." [19]

Whoever examines the broad reach of Duhamel's publications — ignoring, if he wishes, the additional subjects treated in the memoirs of the Academy and his annual reports on meteorology conditions observed at Denainvilliers — cannot fail to be impressed, especially if he recalls that they were productions of years after his fifty-eighth birthday and prior to his death at eighty-two. Generous in his actions (as in the revision and publication in the *Descriptions* of the studies by Réaumur), almost invariably interested with observations and explication alone, not with efforts to modify public policy, and active all his days in the pursuit of knowledge and in its broadcast to those who might

[17] Duhamel's ability was well recognized in his life time by Panckoucke, for the latter often speaks of him and his works with praise in the *Supplément* to the *Encyclopédie*. For example, it is said in t. 2, p. 503: "M. Duhamel, whose descriptions are so exact, so methodical, and so clear," and again in t. 4, p. 375: "It is he (Duhamel) whom we are going to take as guide (for the art of making pipes); we could not follow a better one."

[18] Young, Arthur, *Travels in France* (1889 edition), pp. 80–81.

[19] Marshall, T. H., "Jethro Tull's 'New Husbandry'," *Economic history review*, v. 2 (1929–30), pp. 51–52.

put it to practical use, Duhamel du Monceau presents a figure of the truly benign scientist such as one encounters all too rarely in cultural history.

## THE DESCRIPTIONS THEMSELVES

Those familiar with the modern richness, if not plethora of books descriptive of technological processes, might fail at first blush to be impressed by the *Descriptions des arts et métiers*. A brief research would suggest to them the novelty of the work and the courage of the Academy in embracing the task of preparing it. The only previous publications that resembled it were really but acorns to the Academy's full-blown oak. There were early picture books, such as Schopper's *Panoplia*, published in Frankfurt in 1568, or Garzoni's *Piazza universale*, first issued in Italy in 1585. Savary Des Brulons' *Dictionnaire universel de commerce* (published in three volumes, 1723–1730, with various subsequent editions) had carried a good deal on industrial products and a little upon the processes of their creation. And again there had been quite an amount written in the fields of mining and metallurgy (which are in considerable measure covered in the *Descriptions*), from Agricola's *De Re Metallica* (1556) down through the seventeenth and early eighteenth centuries. In England, there is almost nothing upon technical processes of production in John Harris' *Lexicon technicum* (2 vols., 1704–10), while not much more appeared in Ephraim Chambers' *Cyclopaedia, or an universal dictionary of arts and sciences* (2 vols., 1727).

Curiously enough, however, the English appear to have had somewhat the same idea as the Royal Academy of Sciences — and had begun to carry it out earlier than the French. The Royal Society of London had been founded in 1660 — six years before the Académie Royale des Sciences was set up formally in Paris — and, as early as 1667, Thomas Spratt reports that "histories" (meaning descriptions) of various industrial processes had been prepared by members of that Society and had been "brought in": iron-making, leather dressing, masonry, tin-working, etc.[21] Sir William Petty delivered a "history" in November, 1661, pertaining to "making cloth with sheepswool" and one in May, 1662, related to "the common practices of dyeing"; while the distinguished John (?) Evelyn, between 1662 and 1665, presented data on producing marbled paper on the rolling press, chalcography, and the several manners of making bread in France.[22]

Indeed, other papers seem to have been submitted to the Society on topics of this character through the first few decades of the institution's career.[23] Then something happened. At the time when the 'theoretical French' under

[21] Spratt, Thomas, *The history of the Royal Society of London for the Improving of Natural Knowledge*, (London, 1667), pp. 253 *seq.*
[22] Birch, Thomas, *The history of the Royal Society* . . . (London, 1756–67), v. 1, pp. 55, 69, 83, and 85; and v. 2, p. 19.
[23] See Spratt, *op. cit.*, 2d ed. (1702), *passim*; Birch, *op. cit.*; Johnson, E. A. J., *Predecessors of Adam Smith* (New York, 1937), Appendix A; and Lyons, Sir Henry, *The Royal Society, 1660–1680* (Cambridge, Eng., 1944), p. 130.

the influence of the Abbé Bignon and M. de Réaumur were reviving the Academy's interest in handicrafts, the 'practical British' turned more "academic," attracted by the achievements registered in mathematics and physics.[24] Really not until the formation of another body, the Society of Arts, in 1753, did English interest in technological matters again have an effective focal point — and by that time Réaumur was well advanced with the French project.

Not only was the English movement short-lived, but in a very real sense it was fruitless. A few "histories," it is true, were printed in the *Philosophical transactions* of the Royal Society (or Birch's volumes, which were something of a supplement to the *Transactions*); but this form of publication would hardly lead to wide popular consumption. Other papers seem to have been merely "registered" with the Society, and then buried in the archives. Again, it may be contended that the English productions were the result of individual inquiries or research, not that of organized group action, and that, viewed as a whole, they covered much less ground than the *Descriptions*. In most respects, then, and surely in its over-all magnitude and thoroughness, there was nothing earlier that stands worthy comparison with the output of the Académie Royale des Sciences.

The spirit in which the Academy and its members set about their task is no less noteworthy: the work should be based on the practices observed in actual production, although, to be sure, the best methods there found; the research should inure wholly to the public good and especially to that of the practitioners of the arts and handicrafts — who, in fact, often might resist improvement in their methods; and the series should not only draw upon all talent, domestic and foreign, but should be published despite the trepidations of those who feared enhanced competition from foreign manufacturers.

To be sure, there was the expression from time to time of a hope that the scientists of the Academy could contribute to the solution of technical difficulties which had blocked the progress of particular industries, and that they might be helpful in transmitting improvements from one branch of manufacture to another; but the main emphasis was always on description and not improvement, except in so far as the published descriptions of the better methods and equipment might, as it were, bring the laggards up to par. When the Academy was reviving its project in 1759, mere practitioners of various arts and handicrafts — not necessarily scientists — were solicited as contributors of monographs, especially those who were operators of the more sizable manufacturing establishments then existent in France. Indicative of the situation is the fact that six authors of individual monographs in the series have never been fully identified. For example, they appear in the catalogue of the Bibliothèque Nationale as "M. Dudin" or "M. Paulet." Some of the authors are specified in their several volumes to be "director of an indigo manufactory for many years," or "merchant potter of Chartres," or just "master carpenter."

[24] Lyons, *op. cit.*, pp. 130, 154, and 181–82.

Again, the academicians, like Duhamel du Monceau, took pains to acknowledge aid from practical men of affairs. The latter speaks of "memoirs and instructions from M. de Noinville, erstwhile director of the royal carpet manufactory of Chaillot"; and M. de Lalande in his description of papermaking speaks of his indebtedness to M. de Melie, who had long been one of the proprietors of a manufactory at Mount Magis. All through the collection indeed there are obvious efforts to base the several descriptions upon the then current practices in the more progressive enterprises of the country.

The attainment of accurate delineations of the best handicraft practices then in vogue was indeed essential for one of the purposes that lay beyond this effort. Arts and handicrafts were born in obscurity and had advanced but slowly from century to century in the past, according to the Academy's *Avertissement général*, published, as seen above, at the beginning of the series' appearance; and one of the chief authors, M. de Lalande, sought to explain this slowness as caused by a "jealous fear, a selfish distrust on the part of the workmen who hide, as best they can, the practices and resources of their arts out of a fear of having to share them." For him, as for others, it was part of their hopes that the publication of the *Descriptions* by the Academy might aid to "dispel this secretive obscurity" that surrounded so many of the crafts by bringing to them "the torch of physical science and the spirit of observation."

And another "jealous fear" seems to have disturbed the academicians, that which flowed from the strong nationalism of eighteenth-century France. Surely the French workmen should be encouraged to improve their methods and to get rid of routines based upon unscientific principles, but would not publication of these *Descriptions* allow other countries to copy French methods? M. de Lalande seems to have led the argument against any restriction upon publication arising from this narrow point of view. In his *Art du tanneur* he calls upon the Academy to publish its *Descriptions* "without dissimulation, without restriction, without jealousy. It is more profitable for a country to share with all other peoples the feeble lights which the skill of our workmen may give us, in order to perfect these practices together, than to remain eternally in a state of mediocrity . . . from which they will never extricate themselves alone." [25]

The program on the whole was a simple one. The academicians could with advantage to the country utilize their powers of scientific observation and their fund of scientific knowledge to describe accurately and clearly the methods of operation in the more important manufactures of the country; possibly this increased communication between science and industry would inure directly to the public good through improvements which the scientists might propose; but at least descriptions of the best current practices — especially if the vol-

[25] Lalande, *Art du tanneur*, p. iv. He repeats the same thought in his *Art de faire le papier*, pp. ii–iii. In the latter case, he adds the thought that if France attempted to frustrate the foreigner as far as French practices were concerned, it would also be frustrating its own good citizens.

umes or cahiers were issued individually and at low cost,[26] as the Academy indeed intended — would raise the general level of industrial practice in the country and break through many old traditional but wholly unscientific procedures; and the Academy should not be deterred from its plans because the benefits of its operations would not be confined by the national frontiers.[27]

## THE WORTH OF THE SERIES

As far as the quality of the volumes actually issued is concerned, one is at a handicap in attempting to evaluate techniques which have long since disappeared. Whether M. Demachy gave an adequate, even enlightened description of the art of distilling nitric or other acids or M. Garsault handled effectively the art of the tailor or M. Malouin that of the miller, only experts in the history of these several skills could pass judgement.[28] In terms of quantity, however, surely the output of the Academy exceeds that of any contemporary source. Its nearest competitor was Diderot's *Encyclopédie*, which in fact carried many descriptions of arts and handicrafts and included plates similar to those that were employed by the Academy in all its volumes. But the text in the former is often quite restricted as compared with that found in the Academy's monographs — eleven pages instead of 150 or one page instead of sixty-eight for particular trades — although sometimes the number of engravings in the Diderot volumes of plates exceeds those pertaining to a given craft in the *Descriptions*.

As another basis of judgment, we have the evaluation of contemporaries of the competence of certain contributors to the Academy's publication, and, if imitation is complimentary, it is clear that the *Descriptions* enjoyed a high

[26] This provision is pronounced a success by M. de la Gardette in the preface to his *L'art du plombier et fontainier* of 1773. The artisans could purchase the cahiers separately, he said, and have them bound, thus securing a collection "perfect in its kind" and "far superior to anything which has previously been published."

[27] Actually some parts of particular studies — at least in preliminary form — and investigations of allied subjects formed topics of oral reports (and possibly written memoirs) to the Academy. The contributions of des Billettes and Jaugeon have already been mentioned. In addition one may note Courtivron's discourse in 1747 on the necessity of perfecting the metallurgy of iron-working, Daubenton's report of 1779 on the means of knowing the fineness of wools, or Fougeroux de Bondaroy's memoir of 1785 on the use which could be made of the skins of sea-cows. Probably a good deal of data on French manufacturing techniques beyond those published in the *Descriptions* is to be found in the archives of the Academy. Moureau in his study of *Les Saint-Aubin* (Paris, 1894, pp. 10–11) states that there then existed in the library of the Institut (successor organization to the Academy) a number of essays in the hand-writing of Germain de Saint-Aubin — whom we recognize as author of the *Art du brodeur* in the Academy's series.

[28] That twentieth-century craftsmen are still interested in the processes outlined in the *Descriptions* is indicated by inquiries made to the libraries which own sets of the work. One librarian reports several requests for data on the alum process of tanning as described in Lalande's *Art du tanneur*, another mentions contemporary interest (perhaps merely historical) by paper companies in the same author's *Art de faire le papier*, and another states that Roland de la Platière's treatise on making velour was borrowed and used over a long period of time by an artist engaged in designing upholstery fabrics for American colonial restorations. Organ makers still consult Bedos de Celles frequently. For the opinion of an illustrious eighteenth-century American, one may turn to Dr. Franklin, who, in a letter of May 31, 1788, to James Bowdoin, said of the *Descriptions*: "It is voluminous, well executed, and may be useful in our country."

rating. For example, there is a great similarity between the engravings provided in the *Encyclopédie* and those executed for the treatises of the academicians. So close was the similarity between the two products that the volumes of plates of the Diderot series carry a statement, dated January 16, 1760, to the effect that a committee of the Academy had examined the new items and had "recognized nothing which had been copied from the drawings of M. de Réaumur." Since the Academy followed the style set by Réaumur, this statement means, in substance, that though the *Encyclopédie* utilized an identical method for illustrating industrial processes, it did not use exactly the same drawings and did not copy those which had been devised by the experts of the Academy.

But, although Diderot and his aides were careful not to copy anything feature for feature from the *Descriptions* in the volumes of their plates, editor Panckoucke seems to have felt no such compunctions about borrowing directly from the work of the Academy by the time that he put out his *Nouveau dictionnaire pour servir de supplément, etc.* and his *Suite du receuil de planches* in 1776–1777 and 1777, respectively. In the text he usually made acknowledgment when he printed material based on the *Descriptions*. Sometimes, however, he merely used a statement similar to the following: "See *L'art du cordonnier* by M. de Garsault." Some of his remarks in reference to the treatises upon which he leaned are flattering to the writers of the Academy's series, as seen above [29] and in the following: "M. de Garsault has published an excellent description of the art of the seamstress"; and "we owe to M. le Comte de Milly an excellent description of the art of making porcelain; it is from this scholar that we shall borrow all that we are going to say on this art." [30]

The more flagrant borrowing, however, is to be seen in the plates of the *Supplément*, where, with no statement of the source, parts were lifted from the engravings of the *Descriptions*. (As an example of this plagiarism plates from the two works are reproduced herewith.) [31]

[29] See reference to Duhamel du Monceau, p. 12, note 17, above.

[30] *Supplément*, v. 3, p. 752, and v. 4, p. 506, respectively.

[31] For further examples, see plates 113, 114, and 215 of the *Suite du receuil, etc.* and compare them with plates one and two of the *Art du cirier*, plates 1, 2, and 3 of *L'art de faire différentes sortes de colles*, and plates 3 and 5 of *L'art du tailleur*, respectively. For other borrowings, see the plates dealing with porcelain and pipes, among others, in the two publications.

For data upon this matter of plagiarism, see *Année littéraire*, 1759, v. 7, p. 341, and 1760, v. 1, p. 246. Also see Huard, Georges, *Diderot et L'Encyclopédie: Exposition commemorative du deuxième centenaire de l'Encyclopédie*, (Paris, Bibliothèque Nationale, 1951), pp. xv–xvi, and 13–15.

The *Année littéraire* for 1760 contains Pierre Patte's letter to the editor, dealing with a report that had been signed by six members of the Academy of Sciences — including Morand, Lalande, and Abbé Nollet — in which the claim was made that some forty of Réaumur's engravings had been "in the hands" of the editors of *Encyclopédie*. Again, J. H. S. Formey, secretary of the Académie de Prusse, published in his *Souvenirs d'un citoyen de Berlin* (1789), v. 2, p. 169, a letter written to him by Réaumur on February 23, 1756, in which he complained of "the theft which had been made" of his engravings by "some little-delicate persons," who had had them reengraved for use in the *Dictionnaire Encyclopédique*. Georges Huard, editor of the catalogue of the *Bibliothèque Nationale* exhibit on the *Encyclopédie* — containing ten items dealing with the *Descriptions* — refers to this incident in his introduction and states, "Certainly Réaumur exag-

That the competence of certain scholars who were later to contribute to the *Descriptions* was early recognized by the editors of the *Encyclopédie* is evident from the fact that their collaboration was sought by them. Paul-Jacques Malouin, for instance, was one of the original "encyclopédistes," being charged with the articles on chemistry.[32] Pierre-Charles Le Monnier also contributed several articles to the early volumes of Diderot's publication.[33] And, later on, when the *Supplément* to the *Encyclopédie* was issued, M. Lalande was commissioned by Panckoucke to revise and complete the articles on astronomy.[34]

Again, in any appraisal of the worth of the series, imitation in the form of translations "with comments" should be mentioned. Many items of the cahiers issued by the Academy were translated quickly into German and published in twenty volumes under the title, *Schauplatz der Künste und Handwerke*, between 1762 and 1795.[35] These volumes are described as large quarto. If so, the engravings must have been redrawn and re-executed.

A Swiss printing was also carried through soon after the Academy's cahiers appeared in Paris. The editor, Jean-Élie Bertrand, professor of belles-lettres at Neufchâtel, and member of the Academy of Sciences of Munich and of the Society of the Curious of Nature of Berlin, was himself particularly enthusiastic about the material which he was reprinting. In his preface, he writes: "Since the invention of printing, I do not believe that anyone has formed a more important or more useful project than that of the gentlemen of the Royal Academy of Sciences . . . Their venture marks a memorable epoch in the history of the crafts. It makes illustrious our century. It does honor to France, where one has had the courage to formulate it. It will endear to the most remote posterity the names of the scholars who have generously consecrated their talents and labors to it." Like the German edition, this series was in large quarto dimensions, a format "much easier to handle" than that of

gerates. None of the plates of *Encyclopédie*, it seems, reproduced to a T any of his, but all are greatly inspired by those of his draftsmanship." Pierre Grosclaude, in *Un audacieux Message*, *L'Encyclopédie* (Paris, Nouvelles Éditions Latines, 1951, p. 97, footnote 1), reviews the bases of this accusation, and concludes: "In spite of the acquittal [by the Academy] we are inclined to believe today that the *Encyclopédie* did indeed plagiarize a certain number of the plates . . . ; certain similarities are too striking . . . " This statement obviously refers to the plates of the Diderot volumes, and not to those of the *Supplément*.

[32] See *Encyclopédie*, v. 1, p. 97, 118, and 501.

[33] See *Encyclopédie*, v. 1, p. 214, v. 6, p. 616. Another contributor to the Academy's work, Jean-R. Perronet, wrote the article "Pompes à Feu" in v. 5 of the *Encyclopédie*.

[34] See *Supplément*, v. 1, p. i for Panckoucke's estimate of Lalande as the "author of the most instructive and most complete work that we have on astronomy."

[35] Kayser's *Vollständiges Bücher-Lexicon* (v. 5, p. 61) gives the editors and the places of publication. Some volumes were printed in Königsberg, some in Nürnberg, and the latter volumes in Berlin. As a matter of fact, a twenty-first volume was issued in 1805, but this seems to be wholly a German product, not a translation from the French. The translators were Johann Heinrich Gottlob von Justi (first four volumes), Daniel Gottfried Schreber (volumes 5–15), J. C. Halle and G. C. Rosenthal (volumes 16–20). Not all the titles of the original printings were included. In 1832 a new German series, *Neuer Schauplatz der Künste und Handwerke*, was initiated. As indicated below (p. 20), a translation of *L'art du facteur d'orgues* appears in this series.

the Paris printing, according to Bertrand. Furthermore, the price was less than that of the original edition which, says the editor, had been executed with a luxury which was quite "useless," were it not for the fact that certain wealthy people and some libraries were able to pay the high price for the "superbly printed" Academy edition. It was Bertrand's plan to group together in volumes the related treatises, such as all those which dealt with the manufacture of food stuffs or those pertaining to leather working. This praiseworthy practice was carried out in many of the nineteen volumes, but (as will be noted in Appendix B) Bertrand was not able to follow it completely, especially in the final numbers of his publication.

The high quality of the material contained in the *Descriptions* is also suggested likewise by translations and reprintings other than those intended to involve the whole series issued by the Academy. Gabriel Jars' *Art de fabriquer la brique et la tuile en Hollande* was re-translated from Schreber's German version into Polish and published in Warsaw in 1776; Lalande's *Art de faire le papier* and his *Art du tanneur* appeared in Dutch in 1792 and in English in 1773, respectively; Spanish and Arabic translations of Macquer's *Art de la teinture en soie* were printed in 1771 and 1823; Galon's *Art de convertir le cuivre rouge en laiton* was issued in Spanish translation in 1779; Duhamel's *L'art du charbonnier* had a Portuguese translation in 1801; Demachy's *L'art du distillateur d'eaux-fortes* was published in German in 1784; while Garsault's *Art du paumier-raquetier* appeared in English translation in 1938. Again, numerous reissues are recorded. For example, J. E. Bertrand put out new editions of the following: Duhamel's *Art de rafiner le sucre* (1812), *Art du cirier* (1818 and 1826), *L'art du savonnier* (1819), *Fabrique de l'amidon* (1820); and Demachy's *L'art du distillateur liquoriste* (1819). A new edition of Perret's *L'art du coutelier* was issued in Alançon in 1924–1932, while Roubu's *Art du menuisier* has had some dozen reprintings, in whole or in part, from 1876 to 1930. The item of greatest endurance, however, has been perhaps Dom Bedos de Celles' *L'art du facteur d'orgues*.

The importance of this work on the organ was realized in foreign countries almost immediately. As early as 1779 Johann Samuel Halle, professor of history in the Royal Prussian Corps des Cadets of Berlin, published his *Kunst des Orgelbaues, theoretisch und praktisch beschrieben*, wherein he acknowledges his extensive borrowings from Dom Bedos, analyses the first three parts of the treatise, and suggests that a complete German translation be made. In 1793 Johann Christoph Vollbeding put out in Berlin his *Kurzgefasste Geschichte der Orgel aus dem Französisch des Dom Bedos de Celles*. In a note to this translation of Bedos de Celles' history — which appeared as a preface to the fourth part of his study — Vollbeding characterized *L'art du facteur d'orgues* as the "most complete and most fundamental work of its kind, showing the author's great practical knowledge of organ building." The next adaptation of *The art of the organ builder* was in Dutch, namely, Jan van

Heurn's *De Orgelmaker* (1805–06). This is not a translation of the original, for the author, leaning heavily on Bedos de Celles, included much of his own material. It was not until 1855 that Halle's proposal of a German translation was accomplished. In this year one made by J. S. Topfer was published in his *Lehrbuch der Orgelbaukunst* — which later constituted the 208th volume of the *Neuer Schauplatz der Künste und Handwerke*. But the most important foreign contribution to the distribution and perpetuation of Dom Bedos' study is Christhard Mahrenholz's facsimile edition in two-thirds size, published (four volumes in three) in Kassel from 1934 to 1936, together with a well documented historical statement.[36]

In addition to the foreign publications, there have been two French reprintings of *L'art du facteur d'orgues*. In 1849 and again in 1903 the Librairie Encyclopédique de Roret put out Marie-Pierre Hamel's *Nouveau Manuel complet du facteur d'orgues, ou traité théorique et pratique de l'art de construire les orgues, contenant l'orgue de Dom Bedos et tous les progrès et perfectionnements de la facture jusqu'à ce jour, etc.* In a preface the author, after making a few criticisms of the original, says: "Of all the works written on organ making, that of Dom Bedos holds without contradiction the first place." Because of the clarity of Bedos' descriptions and the rareness of the work, "which is no longer to be had in the trade," Hamel had found it advisable, he says, instead of trying to revise it, to reproduce it "almost literally." [37]

Finally, one may perhaps gain some intimation of the effects wrought by the Academy in its publication efforts by noting the appearance of works somewhat similar in nature, both individual and general. The latter part of the century saw a considerable group of books that presented the art of producing one thing or another. Some of the authors were men connected with the Academy's labors. Thus Roubu, who had covered carpentry in the *Descriptions*, published independently his treatise on the construction of theatres which he had written as a title in the Academy's collection (Paris, 1777); [38] Roland de

[36] This edition is available to American scholars in the following libraries: Congressional, New York Public, University of Chicago, University of California, University of Michigan, Unversity of Pennsylvania, and Yale University School of Music (vol. 1 only).

[37] Dom Bedos' treatise is highly esteemed, as shown by the following statements in 20th century works: J. W. Hinston, *Organ Construction*, London, 1900 (p. 2) "a valuable and exhaustive work" and "this splendid work": Grove's *Dictionary of Music and Musicians*, New York, 1934 (v. 1, p. 256), "an admirable work for the time, and which has remained classical"; Riemann's *Musiklexicon*, Berlin, 1929 (v. 1, p. 133) "a highly significant work." Robert Noehren, University Organist of the University of Michigan says: "It was well-known throughout the 19th century as an important treatise on organ building. However, with the new ideas of the 19th century, its value became more historical than practical. More recently the work has become more and more significant. It sums up to a large extent the technique of organ building in France during the 17th and 18th centuries, perhaps the most important times in the art of organ building. In fact, the years from 1650 to 1725 marked a climax throughout France, Germany and Holland. Today the old organs are being re-discovered, and works like the Dom Bedos are now very important in that they describe the technical details of organ building of that time. I am sure that a translation of it would meet with wide response in all English speaking countries. I am not prepared to say whether or not it is an authentic guide for the modern builder. However, many of its parts are quite applicable to modern organ building." (Letter to G.B.W. of October 21, 1951).

[38] See Appendix A, Addendum.

la Platière's *Art of the peat gatherer* — also intended to form a number of the *Descriptions* — was included in the Neufchâtel quarto edition; while Romme's *Art of the construction, arming, and navigation of vessels* appeared in La Rochelle in 1787. Other works, such as Watin's *Art of making and employing varnish* (Paris, 1772) or Desmaret's *Art of papermaking* (Paris, 1789) seem to have no direct or indirect connection with the Academy's series. The notion of delineating skills extended beyond strictly economic affairs and we find a volume by J. J. Perret (who contributed to the *Descriptions* on the techniques of the cutlery manufacture), which described — presumably with all scientific restraints — the "art" of learning to shave oneself (Paris, 1769)!

Of the efforts to cover the whole field of arts and handicrafts — although not necessarily in exactly the same manner as the Academy of Sciences — it may be noted that the *Descriptions* were scarcely well launched before Philippe Macquer — brother of the author of the series' *Art of silk dyeing* — brought out a two-volume work in Paris entitled *Dictionnaire portatif des arts et métiers*, a publication of enough merit to warrant in 1802 a new edition, "considerably augmented," by the Abbé Pierre Jaubert, in five volumes. In 1782 there began to appear the *Encyclopédie méthodique par order de matières*, known as the Panckoucke reworking with a different plan of the original *Encyclopédie*, of which the section on manufactures (with a volume of 438 plates) was produced by a member of the Academy, and the author of three of its "arts": M. Roland de la Platière.[39] The English were affected: a *Book of trades or library of the useful arts* came out in London in 1804; and George Gregory's more extensive *Dictionary of arts and sciences* was printed in both England and the United States, in 1806 and 1815–16, respectively; while Andrew Ure's famous *Dictionary of arts, manufactures and mines* first appeared in 1839, and continued to be reissued down at least to 1875. The Germans seemingly were most thoroughly infected. A *Neuer Schauplatz der Künste und Handwerke* running to 289 volumes was published in the period 1817–69. This was in no way a reprint of the first *Schauplatz* above-mentioned (which, in turn, had been largely a translation of the Academy's series) but was prepared, with few exceptions, by German writers and, seemingly, endeavored to do for this period of the nineteenth century what the French had envisaged a century before and had begun to publish a half century earlier.[40]

### THE END OF THE ENDEAVOR

Within the Academy itself, the effort to describe the arts and handicrafts of France — after a yearly publication of from four to six items for nearly two decades — suddenly lost its impetus by the latter 1770's. The years prior

[39] Roland de la Platière's work in four volumes, known as *Dictionnaire des manufactures et des arts qui en dépendent*, is prefaced by a preliminary discourse. Another author of the *Descriptions*, Fougeroux de Bondaroy, had been engaged to prepare the articles on woods and forests for the Panckoucke edition, but died before he could complete the task.

[40] As seen above, a translation of Bedos de Celles' *Art du facteur d'orgues* was printed in volume 208 of this publication.

to the Revolution of 1789 were years of meagre production. In fact, from 1780 to 1788 — the date of the last official number of the *Descriptions* — only five new titles were printed.

For this slackening of the Academy's "dry, thorny, and not at all showy" task and its cessation the year preceding the outbreak of the French Revolution, there is no explanation given in the series itself or in the *Histoire* of the Academy, which, from 1761 until 1778, had proudly announced the yearly output of its "arts" to the public, for whom the chore had been "undertaken solely for its utility."

Lacking a definite official statement one is left to theorize and to interpret certain internal evidence. One may infer that the "gentlemen of the Academy" had begun to weary in well doing, that they had preoccupations, that the greater success and lustre of the *Encyclopédie* proved discouraging to them, or that they lost courage because of a realization that their publication was being executed in so elegant a manner that it was too expensive for a wide sale, and too cumbersome to be readily used in the artisans' workshops. The death of the guiding genius and most productive academician, Duhamel du Monceau, in 1782, may have taken away the driving force. And, as the Revolution approached, times became more troubled and the future seemed more uncertain.

As for internal evidence there are important statements in some of the later *Descriptions* and, more important, in two catalogues of the collection which are to be found bound with certain cahiers in some of the extant sets. The first catalogue precedes the preface to Paulet's *L'art du fabricant d'étoffes de soie* (1773). In this list of "the different cahiers which make up the *Descriptions*," three titles are announced as being "in press": *Art de faire les poêles* by Comte de Milly, *Diamantaire* by M. Daubenton, and *Vernisseur* by M. Mittoire. These three titles never appeared in the collection and one may assume that the publishers, fearing an unfavorable reception and light sale, decided to suppress the works even after they had been written, approved, and set up in type. The second catalogue was printed with Lucotte's *L'art de la maçonnerie* (1783). Here appear two important disclosures. In the first place, the publishers announce that the price of the cahiers has been reduced by two-fifths for the individual numbers and by one-half for the entire series. Obviously this statement is to be interpreted to mean that — notwithstanding the fact that some of the cahiers were already out of print and reprintings were being made — the sales had not been in accordance with the hopes of the sponsors of the venture.[41] Secondly, a statement appears as to the most suitable manner in which to bind the individual numbers of the series. This reveals a real weakness in the publishing plan, namely, the printing of the cahiers

---

[41] A new printing of *Art de la teinture en soie* and of *Art du tuilier et du briquetier* is here announced. The items not listed for sale are: *Traité des Pesches* and *La forge des enclumes*.

Ninety-three cahiers are priced, with three in press. Of these the first eighty-six were offered as a set for 640 *livres*. As an example of the price of the individual cahiers, *Charbonnier* was priced at 2 *liv*. 12 *sous* in 1773 and at 1 *liv*. 12 *sous* in 1783.

separately.[42] The printer and bookseller, Moutard, at whose establishment the collection was then to be had, suggested that purchasers bind their copies in the order which "one has followed for the copy of the Royal Academy of Sciences." He indicates fourteen possible volumes, after which he can only state: "The others are not numerous enough on the same matter to be bound." [43]

Finally, in 1788, with the publication of Salmon's *Potier d'étain* — approved by the examiners of the Academy some seven years earlier — the collection was terminated. But, even though the ambitious series of well printed folio volumes had come to an end, a plan to revive the project lingered for at least a decade in the minds of some of the members of the Academy of Sciences. A master apothecary of Paris and manufacturer of chemical products, Antoine Baumé, remembered for his device for determining the alcoholic content of spirits, is reported to have composed more than forty treatises after his attachment to the Academy in 1773: "the art of the perfumer," "the art of the confectioner," "the art of the goldsmith," etc.; [44] but none of these seem to have been printed by the Academy or independently.

The Academy went through difficulties of various sorts in the years following 1789, including its suppression in 1793 along with all the French academies. An organization of the same general character was set up anew in 1795, the Institut National des Sciences et Arts, and apparently some members desired to revive the Academy's project of describing the arts and handicrafts. A resolution of the Institut is reported for 1798 for a program in continuation of the *Descriptions des arts*, and as late as 1800 Citizens Lacepède and Desmarets are recorded in the proceedings of the Institut as being named members of a commission charged with the publication "of the manuscripts and the descriptions of arts and trades." Nothing further happened, however, and the Institut busied itself with other, presumably more fruitful investigations.[45]

The volumes of the *Descriptions des arts et métiers* remain nevertheless a monument to the "gentlemen" of the Académie Royale des Sciences and to the age in France when arts and skills were not only well regarded, but stood still long enough for an all-inclusive portrayal of their methods to be contemplated and carried well toward completion.

[42] The method of printing and selling the cahiers separately is doubtless one of the reasons why librarians have found it so difficult to properly catalogue their collections. As an example of the confused manner in which some sets are bound, one may take a volume from the John Adams set of Harvard. One volume contains the following treatises: *Art du charbonnier, Fabrique des ancres, Art du chandelier, Art de l'épinglier, Art de faire le papier, Art des forges et fourneaux à fer, Art de tirer des carrières la pierre d'ardoise*, etc., and *Art du cirier*. The Franklin set is arranged more logically, the several volumes usually containing related titles.

[43] See above, p. 4, note 4.

Another interesting and important piece of internal evidence is seen in Roubu's *Art du menuisier*, where, in conclusion, it is stated: "One of the great obstacles that I have had to surmount is the cry of the public against the large books, which one does not buy because they are too expensive, or that others buy and do not read because they are too voluminous."

[44] Maury, L. F. A., *L'ancienne Académie des Sciences* (1864), pp. 173-174.

[45] The catalogue of the British Museum lists a quarto *Traité de l'art du charpentier, pour faire suite aux arts et métiers, publiés par l'Académie des Sciences* (1804) by J. B. Hassenfratz.

The many volumes remain also a source of information to the student of eighteenth-century French industry and the background of current manufacturing techniques whether in France or in other countries. Nowhere else are the descriptions of technical processes of handicraftsmanship to be found in any corresponding magnitude, while — as already noted — one will find scattered through the volumes items of more specialized character, such as notes upon the commerce of that period in particular commodities or definitions of terms used in the several French trades of the day. The series inspired by Réaumur and Duhamel du Monceau and executed under the auspices of the Academy of Sciences deserves richly to be rescued from the shadows into which most American libraries have consigned it, and from dusty shelves to a a place of honor among their rare collections. The individual titles should be treated and catalogued as separate volumes, and the whole brought to the attention of students working in special industrial fields as well as in the history of French eighteenth-century development.

APPENDIX A

Beauvais-Raseau, —— de
L'art de l'indigotier.
[Paris], L. F. Delatour, 1770.
1 p.l., 118 p., 11 pl.

Bedos de Celles, [Dom François], *Bénédictin*
L'art du facteur d'orgues.
Première partie: Connoissance de l'orgue & des principes de sa méchanique.
[Paris], L. F. Delatour, 1766.
1 p.l., 142 p., pl. 1–52.
Seconde partie: Pratique de la construction de l'orgue.
N.p., no printer, 1770.
1 p.l., pp. [1, i.e., 143–476].
Troisième partie.
[Paris], L. F. Delatour, 1770.
pp. 477–536, pl. 53–79.
Quatrième partie.
[Paris], L. F. Delatour, 1778.
1 p.l., xxxii, pp [537]–676, pl. 80–137.

Bouchu, ——, *see* Courtivron, Art des forges.

Chapman, Fredrik [Henrik]
Traité de la construction des vaisseaux, avec une explication où l'on démontre les principes de l'architecture navale marchande, & des navires armés en course. Traduit du suédois, sur l'édition publiée & imprimée chez Jean Pfeiffer en 1775.*
Paris, Saillant & Nyon [and] Veuve Desaint, 1779. [Colophon gives Ph.-D. Pierres, 1779.]
1 p.l., viii, 165, [1] p., 11 pl., with 8 pl. of *règles* and *dimensions*.

Chaulnes, Michel-Ferdinand d'Albert d'Ailly, duc de
Description d'un microscope, et de différents micromètres destinés à mesurer des parties circulaires ou droites, avec la plus grande précision.
[Paris], L. F. Delatour, 1768.
1 p.l., 18 p., 6 pl.
Nouvelle méthode pour diviser les instruments de mathématique et d'astronomie.
[Paris], L. F. Delatour, 1768.
1 p.l., 44 p., 15 pl.

Courtivron, Gaspard Le Compasseur-Créquy-Montfort, M[arquis] de
Art des forges et fourneaux à fer, par M[onsieur] le marquis de Courtivron et par M[onsieur] Bouchu.
Première section: Des mines de fer, et de leurs préparations.
N.p., no printer, n.d.
1 p.l., 66 p., 4 pl.
Seconde section: Du feu appliqué au travail du fer.
N.p., no printer, n.d.
31 p., 2 pl.

* The Swedish title is *Traktat om Skepps-Byggeriet, tillika med förklaring och bevis ofver architectura navalis mercatoria.* . . . Stockholm, 1775.

Troisième section; Quatrième moyen de l'art du feu appliqué au travail du fer.*
[Paris], H. L. Guérin & L. F. Delatour, 1762.
141 p., 16 pl.
Suite de la troisième section: Nouvel art d'adoucir le fer fondu et de faire des ouvrages
    de fer aussi finis que de fer forgé, par M[onsieur] de Réaumur [with an introduc-
    tion by Duhamel du Monceau].
N.p., no printer, 1762.
[i]–viii, 124 p., 7 pl.
Quatrième section: Traité du fer, par M[onsieur] Swedemborg [sic]: traduit du Latin
    par M[onsieur] Bouchu.**
N.p., no printer, 1762.
1 p.l., [2], 196 p., 9 pl.
See also Duhamel du Monceau, Art du couvreur.

Demachy, Jacques-François
L'art du distillateur d'eaux-fortes, &c.
[Paris], L. F. Delatour, 1773.
1 p.l., iv, 198 p., 12 pl.
    Introduction: pp. 1–2.
    Première partie: De la préparation des eaux-fortes & autres acides: pp. 3–46.
    Seconde partie: De la préparation en grand des produits chimiques fluides: pp.
      47–100.
    Troisième partie: De la préparation en grand des produits chimiques solides: pp.
      101–178.
    Explication des planches [and] supplément: pp. 179–198.
L'art du distillateur liquoriste, contenant le brûleur d'eaux-de-vie, le fabriquant de
    liqueurs, le débitant ou le cafetier-limonadier.
N.p., no printer, 1775.
[i]–x, 153 p., 16 pl.
    Introduction: pp. 1–5.
    Première partie: De l'art du brûleur ou bouilleur d'eau-de-vie: pp. 6–54.
    Seconde partie: Du fabriquant de liqueurs ou du distillateur liquoriste proprement
      dit: pp. 55–107.
    Troisième partie: Du débitant de liqueurs, plus connu sous la dénomination de
      cafetier-limonadier: pp. 108–132.
    Explication des planches [etc.]: pp. 133–153.

Dengenoust, ——, see Duhamel du Monceau, Art du charbonnier.

Dudin, ——.
L'art du relieur-doreur de livres.
[Paris], L. F. Delatour, 1772.
1 p.l., iv, 112 p., 16 pl.

Duhamel du Monceau, Henri-Louis
L'art de faire différentes sortes de colles.
N.p., no printer, 1771.
1 p.l., 27 p., 3 pl.
Art de faire les tapis, façon de Turquie, connus sous le nom de tapis de la Savonnerie

  * This part carries the preliminary note:
    "Cette section & les deux premières ont été dressées sur le plan, la révision, les retranche-
    ments, les corrections & les changements de M. le Marquis de Courtivron, par M. Bouchu,
    qui y a fait entrer une partie des différents mémoires qu'il avoit précédemment adressés à
    M. de Malesherbes, premier président de la Cour des Aides, en y joignant tout ce qui a
    été extrait des papiers de M. de Réaumur, & toutes les planches gravées que M. de Courti-
    vron lui a communiquées."
  ** Emmanuel Swedenborg, *Regnum subterraneum sive minerale de ferro. . .* , published as the
second volume of his *Opera philosophica et mineralia*, Dresden and Leipzig, 1734.

[sur les mémoires & instructions de M[onsieur] de Noinville, ancien Directeur de la Manufacture Royale de Chaillot].

[Paris, L. F. Delatour], 1766.

1 p.l., 25 p., 4 pl.

L'art de faire les pipes à fumer le tabac.

[Paris], L. F. Delatour, 1771.

1 p.l., 34, p., 11 pl.

Art de friser ou ratiner les étoffes de laine.

[Paris], L. F. Delatour, 1766.

1 p.l., 10 p., 5 pl.

Art de la draperie, principalement pour ce qui regarde les draps fins.

[Paris], H. L. Guérin & L. F. Delatour, 1765.

1 p.l., 150 p., 15 pl.

Art de rafiner le sucre.

N.p., no printer, 1764.

1 p.l., 78 p., 10 pl.

Art de réduire le fer en fil connu sous le nom de fil d'archal.

[Paris], L. F. Delatour, 1768.

1 p.l., 32 p., 5 pl.

Art du cartier.

N.p., no printer, 1762.

1 p.l., 38 p., 5 pl.

Art du chandelier.

N.p., no printer, 1764.

1 p.l., 41 p., 3 pl.

Art du charbonnier, ou manière de faire le charbon de bois.

N.p., no printer, n.d.*

30 p., 1 pl.

> Additions et corrections relatives à l'Art du charbonnier: Détails sur la consomma-
> tion du charbon pour les forges et fourneaux à fer: par M[onsieur] Dengenoust,
> capitaine en premier au corps Royal d'Artillerie, avec des réflexions utiles pour
> l'exploitation des Mines de fer, et des Tentatives pour y employer du Charbon de
> houille.
>
> N.p., no printer, [1770?].
>
> 13 p.

Art du cirier.

[Paris], H. L. Guérin & L. F. Delatour, 1762.

1 p.l., 113 p., 8 pl.

Art du couvreur. [Including observations upon "couvertures en lave," pp. 41–48, by
    Courtivron.]

[Paris], L. F. Delatour, 1766.

1 p.l., 56 p., 4 pl.

Art du potier de terre.

[Paris], L. F. Delatour, 1773.

1 p.l., 84 p., 17 pl.

Art du savonnier.

[Paris], L. F. Delatour, 1774.

1 p.l., 70 p., 6 pl.

Art du serrurier.

* This is the first unit in the *Descriptions des Arts et Métiers* and is preceded by a general
title-page for the whole series which bears the data: Paris, Desaint & Saillant, Libraires, rue Saint
Jean de Beauvais, 1761. Avec Approbation & Privilège du Roi. It is also preceded by an *Avertissement*, probably by Duhamel du Monceau. Morand in *L'art d'exploiter les mines de charbon de
terre*, pp. 1,611–1,612, says that this was published in 1759 and inserted before the *Art du charbonnier*.

[Paris], L. F. Delatour, 1767.
1 p.l., iii, 302 p., 42 pl.
L'art du tuilier et du briquetier, par M[essieurs] Duhamel [du Monceau], Fourcroy
[de Ramecourt], & Gallon [sic].
N.p., no printer, 1763.
1 p.l., 67 p., 9 pl.
    [Suite]: Art de fabriquer la brique et la tuile en Hollande, et de les faire cuire avec
la tourbe, pour servir de suite à l'Art du Tuilier et du Briquetier. Par M[onsieur] Jars.
[Paris], L. F. Delatour, 1767.
11 p., 1 pl. [numbered "X"].
De la forge des enclumes.
[Paris], H. L. Guérin & L. F. Delatour, 1762.
1 p.l., 11 p., 1 pl.
Fabrique de l'amidon.
[Paris], L. F. Delatour, 1772.
1 p.l., 11 p., 1 pl.

Traité général des pesches, et histoire des poissons qu'elles fournissent, tant pour la
subsistance des hommes, que pour plusieurs autres usages qui ont rapport aux arts et au
commerce. . . [Caption titles carry]: Traité des pêches, et histoire des poissons, ou des
animaux qui vivent dans l'eau. Paris, Saillant & Nyon [and] Desaint, 1769 [on general title-
page].
    [Première partie.]
        [Tome I]
            Première section: De la pesche aux hameçons. Conjectures sur l'invention de
                cette pesche.
            [Paris], L. F. Delatour, 1769.
                2 p.l., 84 p., 21 pl.
            Seconde section: Des filets; et des différentes façons de les employer pour
                plusieurs sortes de pêches.
            N.p., no printer, [1770?].
                1 p.l., 66, [1] p., 20 pl.
            Suite de la seconde section:
                N.p., no printer, [1770?].
                1 p.l., pp. 67–192, pl. 21–50.
            Troisième section: Où l'on traite de plusieurs façons de pêcher qui n'ont pu
                être rapportées à celles dont nous avons parlé dans les deux précédentes
                sections; avec quelques discussions qui sans appartenir proprement aux
                pêches, y ont un rapport très prochain.
            [Paris], L. F. Delatour, 1771.
                1 p.l., 140 p., 15 pl.
    Seconde partie.
        Paris, Saillant & Nyon [and] Desaint, 1772 [on title-page].
        [Tome II]
            Introduction [and] première section: De la morue, et des poissons qui y ont
                rapport.
            [Paris], L. F. Delatour, 1772.
                2 p.l., 180 p., 27 pl.
            Seconde section: Du saumon, et des poissons qui y ont rapport.
            N.p., no printer, [1773?].
                1 p.l., pp. 181–314, 17 pl.
            Troisième section: De l'alose, et des poissons qui y ont rapport.
            N.p., no printer, [1776].
                1 p.l., pp. 315–488, 22 pl.
            Suite de la troisième section:
                [Paris], L. F. Delatour, 1776.
                1 p.l., pp. 489–579, pl. 23–31.

Suite de la seconde partie.
   Paris, Saillant & Nyon [and] Veuve Desaint, 1777 [on title-page].
   Tome III
      Quatrième section: Caractères généraux des poissons . . . que nous nommons
         Sparus comme dénomination générique.
         [Paris], L. F. Delatour, 1777.
         2 p.l., 82 p., 15 pl.
      Cinquième section: D'une famille de poissons qu'on nomme Zeus.
         [Paris], L. F. Delatour, 1778.
         1 p.l., pp. 83–130, 11 pl.
      Sixième section: Dans laquelle nous parlerons des poissons qui ont sur le dos
         deux ailerons bien distincts.
         [Paris], L. F. Delatour, 1778.
         1 p.l., pp. [131]–164, 5 pl.
      Septième section: Des scombres, *Scomber* ou *Scombrus*.
         [Paris], J. Ch. Desaint, 1779.
         1 p.l., pp. [165]–217, 9 pl.
      Huitième section: De l'esturgeon, *Acipenser*, *Sturio*, et des poissons qui y ont
         rapport.
         [Paris], J. Ch. Desaint, 1779.
         1 p.l., pp. [219–252], 7 pl.
      Neuvième section: Des poissons plats.
         [Paris], J. Ch. Desaint, [1780?].
         1 p.l., pp. [253]–326, 8 pl.
      Suite de la neuvième section: Addition à ce que nous avons dit sur plusieurs
         poissons dont il a été parlé dans la neuvième Section.
         N.p., no printer, [1781?].
         pp. 327–336, pl. 9–27.
   Tome IV
   Paris, Veuve Desaint, 1782 [on title-page].
      Dixième section: Des poissons cetacées, et des amphibies.
         [Paris], J. Ch. Desaint, [1782?].
         1 p.l., 73 p., 15 pl.
*See also* Courtivron, Art des forges; Galon; and Réaumur.


Fougeroux d'Angerville, ——, *see* Lalande, Art de faire le parchemin.


Fougeroux de Bondaroy, Auguste-Denis
   Art de tirer des carrières la pierre d'ardoise, de la fendre et de la tailler.
   N.p., no printer, [1762?].
   [i]–iv, 66 p., 4 pl.
   Art de travailler les cuirs dorés ou argentés.
   [Paris], H. L. Guérin & L. F. Delatour, 1762.
   1 p.l., 42 p., 2 pl.
   L'art du coutelier en ouvrages communs.
   [Paris], L. F. Delatour, 1772.
   [i]–iv, 58 p., 7 pl.
   Art du tonnelier.
   [Paris], H. L. Guérin & L. F. Delatour, 1763.
   1 p.l., 68 p., 6 pl.


Fourcroy de Ramecourt, Charles-René
   Art du chaufournier.
   N.p., no printer, 1766.
   1 p.l., 74 p., 15 pl.
   *See also* Duhamel du Monceau, Art du tuilier et du briquetier.

Galon, *colonel d'infanterie*

  L'art de convertir le cuivre rouge ou cuivre de rosette, en laiton ou cuivre jaune, au moyen de la pierre calaminaire; de le fondre en tables; de le battre sous le martinet & de le tirer à la filière.

  pp. 1–44.

  Avertissement de M[onsieur] Duhamel [du Monceau], chargé de suivre l'impression du Mémoire de M. Gallon [*sic*]: [and] Extrait de ce que Swedenborg a rapporté sur la calamine, & la conversion de la Rosette en Laiton, dans un ouvrage latin, intitulé: le Regne souterrein ou Minéral [translated by Theodore] Baron [d'Henonville].*

  pp. 45–56.

    Duhamel du Monceau, Henri-Louis

    De la fonte et de l'affinage du cuivre et du potin, à Ville-Dieu-les-Poëles en Normandie.

    pp. [57]–70.

    Addition au travail du cuivre; ou description de la manufacture du cuivre de M[onsieur] Raffaneau, établie près d'Essone.

    pp. 71–74.

  N.p., no printer, 1764.

  1 p.l., 78 p., 18 pl.

  Explication des figures: pp. 75–78.

  *See also* Duhamel du Monceau, Art du tuilier et du briquetier.


Garsault, François-A[lexandre-Pierre] de

  L'art de la lingère.

  [Paris], L. F. Delatour, 1771.

  1 p.l., 58 p., 4 pl.

  L'art du bourrelier et du sellier.

    N.p., no printer, 1774.

    1 p.l., 147 p., 15 pl.

    Première section: Du bourrelier-bâtier: pp. 9–68.

    Seconde section: Du bourrelier-carrossier: pp. 69–94.

    L'art du sellier: pp. 95–137.

    Explication des planches: pp. 138–147.

  Art du cordonnier.

  N.p., no printer, 1767.

  [i]–vi, 51 p., 5 pl.

  Art du paumier-raquetier et de la paume.

  N.p., no printer, 1767.

  [i]–iv, 34 p., 5 pl.

  Art du perruquier, contenant la façon de la barbe, la coupe des cheveux, la construction des perruques d'hommes et de femmes, le perruquier en vieux et le baigneur-étuviste.

  N.p., no printer, 1767.

  [i]–vi, 44 p., 5 pl.

  Art du tailleur, contenant le tailleur d'habits d'hommes; les culottes de peau, le tailleur de corps de femmes et enfants, la couturière, et la marchande de modes.

  [Paris], L. F. Delatour, 1769.

  1 p.l., 60 p., 1 l., 16 pl.


Hellot, Jean, *see* Macquer, Art de la teinture en soie.


Hulot, *père*

  L'art du tourneur mécanicien.

  [Paris], L. F. Delatour, 1775.

  [i]–viii, 390 p., 44 pl.

  * Emmanuel Swedenborg, *Regnum subterraneum sive minerale de cupro et orchalco*, published as the third volume of his *Opera philosophica et mineralia*, already cited.

Jars, Gabriel, *see* Duhamel du Monceau, Art du tuilier.

[La Gardette, Claude Mathieu de, *abbé*]
    L'art du plombier et fontainier, par M ***.
    [Paris], L. F. Delatour, 1773.
    [i]–xii, 206 p., 24 pl.

Lalande, [Joseph] Jérôme Le Français de
    L'art de faire le maroquin.
    N.p., no printer, n.d.
    1 p.l., 26 p., 1 pl.
    Art de faire le papier.
    N.p., no printer, n.d.
    1 p.l., iv, 150 p., 14 pl.
    Art de faire le parchemin.
    [Paris], H. L. Guérin & L. F. Delatour, 1762.
    1 p.l., 52 p., 2 pl.
        [Suite]: Fougeroux d'Angerville, —
            Le criblier, suite du parcheminier.
            N.p., no printer, n.d.
            8 p., 2 pl.
    L'art de l'hongroyeur.
    N.p., no printer, n.d.
    1 p.l., 32 p., 1 pl.
    Art du cartonnier.
    N.p., no printer, 1762.
    1 p.l., 30 p., 1 pl.
    Art du chamoiseur.
    N.p., no printer, 1763.
    1 p.l., 46 p., 4 pl.
    Art du corroyeur.
    [Paris], L. F. Delatour, 1767.
    1 p.l., 64 p., 2 pl.
    Art du mégissier.
    [Paris], L. F. Delatour, 1765.
    1 p.l., 48 p., 2 pl.
    Art du tanneur.
    [Paris], H. L. Guérin & L. F. Delatour, 1764.
    [i]–viii, 135 p., 3 pl.

Le Monnier, Pierre-Charles
    Description et usage des principaux instruments d'astronomie [où l'on traite de leur
stabilité, de leur fabrique, et de l'art de les diviser].
    N.p., no printer, 1774.
    [i]–iv, 60 p., 14 pl.

Le Vieil, Pierre
    L'art de la peinture sur verre et de la vitrerie.
    [Paris], L. F. Delatour, 1774.
    [i]–xiv, 245 p., 13 pl.
        Première partie: De la peinture sur verre considérée dans sa partie historique: pp.
            1–94.
        Seconde partie: De la peinture sur verre considérée dans sa partie chimique & mé-
            chanique: pp. 95–198.
        Troisième partie: De l'art de peindre sur verre: pp. 199–239.
        Explication des planches: pp. 241–245.

Lucotte, J. R., *architecte*
    L'art de la maçonnerie.
    Paris, Moutard, 1783.
    38 p., 17 pl.

Macquer, Pierre-Joseph
    Art de la teinture en soie.* [Includes Hellot, —, Procédés particuliers, tirés du dépôt
       du conseil: pp. 71–78.]
    N.p., no printer, 1763.
    [i]–ix, 86 p., 6 pl.
        Explication des figures: pp. 79–83.
        Explication de quelques termes, etc.: pp. 83–86.

Malouin, Paul-Jacques
    Description et détails des arts du meunier, du vermicelier et du boulenger, avec une
    histoire abrégée de la boulengerie et un dictionnaire de ces arts.**
    N.p., no printer, 1767.
    [i]–iv, 340 p., 10 pl.

Morand, Jean-François-Clément
    L'art d'exploiter les mines de charbon de terre.
        Première partie: Du charbon de terre et de ses mines.
           N.p., no printer, 1768.
           1 p.l., xviii, 196 p., 11 pl.
        Seconde partie, première et seconde sections: De l'extraction, de l'usage et du
           commerce du charbon de terre.
           N.p., no printer, 1773.
           1 p.l., pp. [167, i.e., 197]–460, pl. 12 and 13 for the first part, and pl. 1–36
           for the second part.
        Seconde partie, troisième section: Exploitation, commerce et usage du charbon
           de terre en France.
           N.p., no printer, 1774.
           1 p.l., pp. 461–725, 1 unnumbered pl., pl. 37–53.
        Seconde partie, quatrième section: Essai de théorie-pratique sur l'art d'exploiter
           les mines ou carrières de charbon de terre; et sur les différentes manières
           d'employer ce fossile pour les manufactures, atteliers et usages domestiques.
           N.p., no printer, 1776.
           1 p.l., pp. 727–1,114, pl. 54–55.
        Seconde partie, Suite de la quatrième section: Essai de théorie-pratique sur les
           différentes manières d'employer le charbon de terre pour les manufactures,
           atteliers et usages domestiques.
           N.p., no printer, 1777.
           1 p.l., xiii, 1, pp. 1,115–1,356, pl. 56–58: (six plates are numbered 56, nos.
           1 and 2; 57, nos. 1 and 2; 58, and 58 with an asterisk).
        Tables de matières . . . Explication des planches . . . et Additions et corrections.
           N.p., no printer, 1779.
           ii, pp. 1,357–1,612, pl. 58 with two asterisks [belonging to second part].
        Mémoires sur les feux de houille, ou charbon de terre.
           N.p., no printer, n.d.
           44 pp.

Noinville, — de, *see* Duhamel du Monceau, Art de faire les tapis.

Nollet, Jean-Antoine, *abbé*
    L'art de faire des chapeaux.
    N.p., no printer, 1765.
    1 p.l., 94 p., 6 pl.

    * Another later printing is announced in the list presented in Lucotte's Art de la maçonnerie.
    ** Franklin set has an edition of 1779: Nouvelle édition, revue et augmentée.

Paulet, J., *dessinateur & fabriquant en étoffes de soie de la ville de Nîmes.*
  L'art du fabriquant d'étoffes de soie.
      Première et seconde sections: Contenant le dévidage des soies teintes, & l'ourdis-
        sage des chaînes.
        [Paris], L. F. Delatour, 1773.
        Première partie: 3 p.l., l, 34 p., 9 pl.
        Seconde partie: pp. 35–230, 26 pl.
      Troisième et quatrième sections: Contenant l'art du plieur de chaînes & poils
        pour les étoffes de soie unies, rayées & façonnées; & celui de faire les canettes
        pour les étoffes de soie, & les espolins pour brocher.
        [Paris], L. F. Delatour, 1773.
        Troisième partie: 2 p.l., pp. [131]–170, 15 pl.*
        Quatrième partie: pp. [171]–211, 12 pl.
      Cinquième section: Contenant l'art du remisseur ou faiseur de lisses, tant pour
        les étoffes de soie, que pour les autres étoffes, comme draps, toiles, gazes, &c.
        [Paris], L. F. Delatour, 1774.
        1 p.l., pp. [313]–399, 12 pl.*
      Sixième section: Contenant l'art du peigner, ou faiseur de peignes, tant pour la
        fabrique des étoffes de soie, que pour toutes autres étoffes & tissus, comme
        draps, toiles, gazes, &c.
        N.p., no printer, 1775.
        iv, pp. 401–639, 37 pl.
      Septième section, première partie: Contenant la fabrique des taffetas, serges &
        satins unis, & de toutes les étoffes façonnées à la marche & à la petite tire.
        N.p., no printer, 1776.
        1 p.l., 336 p., 33 pl.
      Septième section, suite de la première partie: Contenant la fabrique des taffetas,
        & celle de tous les genres de serges.
        N.p., no printer, 1777.
        1 p.l., pp. 337–544, pl. 34–57.
      Septième section, troisième division de la première partie. Contenant la manière
        de fabriquer les satins unis dans tous les genres et à deux faces, &c; la manière
        de leur donner l'apprêt, ainsi qu'à tous les genres d'étoffes de soie qui en sont
        susceptibles; la manière de fabriquer les étoffes façonnées par la marche
        telles que les taffetas brillantés, les cannelés, les cirsakas dans tous leurs genres;
        les taffetas, gros-de-tours & satins, ainsi façonnés par la marche; les droguets
        ordinaires et à la reine, les prussiennes, les égyptiennes, les amboisiennes et
        les musulmanes.
        [Paris], L. F. Delatour, 1778.
        1 p.l., pp. 545–658 [*i.e.*, 858], pl. 58–90.

Perret, Jean-Jacques
  L'art du coutelier.
  Première partie. La coutellerie proprement dite.
  [Paris], L. F. Delatour, 1771.
  [i]–iv, 239 p., 72 pl.
  L'art du coutelier expert en instruments de chirurgie. Seconde partie de l'art du
    coutelier.
    Première section.
      N.p., no printer, 1772.
      [i]–xii, pp. [241]–374, pl. 73–122.
    Seconde section.
      [Paris], L. F. Delatour, 1772.
      1 p.l., pp. [375]–527, pl. 123–172.

  * There is a break in the pagination between the second and third "sections" and then a com-
pensating one between the fourth and fifth.

Perronet, —, *see* Réaumur, Art de l'épinglier.

Réaumur, René-Antoine Ferchault de
    Art de l'épinglier. Avec des additions de M. Duhamel du Monceau, & des remarques extraites des Mémoires de M[onsieur] Perronet.
        N.p., no printer, n.d.
        77 p., 7 pl.
    Fabrique des ancres, lue à l'Académie en juillet, 1723, par M[onsieur] de Réaumur. Avec des notes et des additions de M. Duhamel [du Monceau].
        N.p., no printer, 1764.
        54 p., 6 pl.
    *See also* Courtivron, Art des forges. Suite de la troisième section.

Roland de la Platière, [Jean-Marie]
    Art de préparer et d'imprimer les étoffes en laines, suivi de l'art de fabriquer les pannes ou peluches, les velours façon d'Utrecht et les moquettes . . .
        Paris, Moutard, 1780.
        21 p. 6 pl.
    L'art du fabricant d'étoffes en laines rases et sèches, unies et croisées . . .
        Paris, Moutard, 1780.
        1 p.l., 62 p., 11 pl.
    L'art du fabricant de velours de coton, précédé d'une dissertation sur la nature, le choix, et la préparation des matières, et suivi d'un traité de la teinture et de l'impression des étoffes de ces mêmes matières.
        Paris, Moutard, 1780.
        2 p.l., ii, 48, [4] p., 11 pl.
            Première partie: pp. 1–32.
            Seconde partie: Contenant les procédés de toutes les couleurs, & la manière de les appliquer sur cette étoffe, ainsi que sur toutes les sortes de toiles, soit à la planche & au cylindre, soit au pinceau: pp. [33]–40.
            Description des planches [&c.], pp. [41]–48 and 4 unnumbered pp.

Romme, [Nicolas] Charles
    L'art de la voilure.
    [Paris], Moutard, 1781.
    68 p., 9 pl.
    Description de l'art de la mâture.
    [Paris], L. F. Delatour, 1778.
    1 p.l., 82 p., 8 pl.

Roubo, [André-Jacob], *fils*
    L'art du layetier.
    Paris, Moutard, 1782.
    28 p., 7 pl.
    L'art du menuisier.
        Première partie: Avant-propos et division de cet ouvrage [and eleven chapters].
        N.p., no printer, 1769.
        1 p.l., [2], 151 p., 50 pl.
        Seconde partie [embracing fourteen chapters].
        [Paris], L. F. Delatour, 1770.
        1 p.l., [2], pp. 153–452, pl. 51–170.
        Troisième partie, première section: L'art du menuisier-carrossier.
        [Paris], L. F. Delatour, 1771.
        1 p.l., pp. 453–598, pl. 171–221.
        Troisième partie, seconde section: L'art du menuisier en meubles.
        [Paris], L. F. Delatour, 1772.
        1 p.l., pp. [599]–762, pl. 222–276.

Troisième partie, troisième section: L'art du menuisier ébéniste.
[Paris], L. F. Delatour, 1774.
1 p.l., pp. 763–1,036, pl. 277–337.
Quatrième et dernière partie: L'art du treillageur ou menuiserie des jardins.
[Paris], L. F. Delatour, 1775.
1 p.l., iv, pp. [1,037]–1,312, pl. 338–382, 107 *bis*.

Saint-Aubin, [Charles Germain] de, *dessinateur du Roi.*
  L'art du brodeur.
  [Paris], L. F. Delatour, 1770.
  1 p.l., 50 p., 10 pl.

Salmon, *marchand potier d'étain.*
  Art du potier d'étain.
  Paris, Moutard, 1788.
  [i–viii], 155 p., 32 pl.

Swedenborg, Emmanuel, *see* Courtivron, Art des forges, and Galon, L'art de convertir le
  cuivre rouge.

Thy, N[icolas] C[hristiern] de, comte de Milly
  L'art de la porcelaine, [dédié au Roi, par M[onsieur] le Comte de Milly, M,DCC,-
  LXXI]. [Mémoire sur la porcelaine d'Allemagne, connue sous le nom de porcelaine de
  Saxe.]
  [Paris], L. F. Delatour, 1771. [Colophon gives 1772.]
  [i]–xxxii, 60, [i] p., 8 pl.

#### Addendum

As pointed out by Brunet in his *Manuel du libraire et de l'amateur de livres* (v. 2, p.
620), there are three items which are sometimes included in this collection, but which do
not necessarily form parts of it. These are: Roubu's *Traité de la construction des théâtres
et des machines théâtrales* (1777), the *Supplément à l'Art du serrurier; ou Essai sur les
combinaisons mécaniques employées particulièrement pour produire l'effet des meilleures
serrures ordinaires* (1781), and Blakey's *Art de faire les ressorts de montres, suivi de la
manière de faire les petits ressorts de répétitions et les ressorts spiraux* (1780). The only
copies of these essays known to be in this country are in Volumes 43, 12, and 43, respectively,
of the set owned by the United States Patent Office.

Roubu's study on the construction of theatres had already been announced by the author
in his *Art du Treillageur* (p. 1,257). He says in his *avertissement* to the first part of his
treatise that he had made it as useful, agreeable, and inexpensive as possible in a format
about similar to that of the Academy series. Because of its nature, however, "this work
cannot be a part of the collection of the arts and trades, but one can hardly refrain from
joining it to the *Art of the Cabinet-maker.*" It was published "with approbation and priv-
ilege of the king" in Paris by Cellot et Joubert fils jeune, rue Dauphine. To show that he
was well documented to make this study, he states that he had consulted, among other
works, *Histoire du Théâtre français* by the Frères Parfaict, *Mélanges d'Histoire et de Lit-
térature* by Voltaire, *Dictionnaire de Musique* by Jean-Jacques Rousseau, and the articles
dealing with the theatres, ancient and modern, in *l'Encyclopédie*. The second part, that
dealing with theatrical machines, seems never to have been published.

The supplement to Duhamel du Monceau's study of the locksmith appears as: *Supplément à l'Art du serrurier; ou Essai sur les combinaisons mécaniques, employées particulièrement pour produire l'effet des meilleures serrures ordinaires, par Joseph Botterman, de
Tilbourg, au pays d'Osterwick, avec figures en taille-douce: ouvrage traduit du hollandais
et utile à tous les serruriers intelligents, publié par M. Feutry de la société philosophique de
Philadelphie*, Paris, Lamy, 1781. Quérard (*op. cit.*, II, p. 655) says that the translator was
supposed to be "un illustre malheureux, l'infortuné Louis XVI"! In the *avis du libraire* of
this essay of 67 pages with five plates, Lamy says that it was being published as "a sort

of supplement to *l'Art du Serrurier*," and that a certain number of copies were being printed without interlines and on a less expensive paper in order that "the workers in this field may more easily acquire it." The approbation was signed at Versailles on May 10, 1780.

Blakey's work on making watch springs was printed by Marc-Michel Rey in Amsterdam in 1780. Blakey, a hydraulic engineer, gives the story of his essay in a long prospectus. Having been encouraged by a member of the Academy "well versed in mechanics," he had composed the first part of his work for the *Descriptions*. This was submitted to the Academy and on September 15, 1772, the examiners, Le Roy and Macquer, gave their approval, judging it "worthy of the approbation of the Academy and of being printed with the arts which it was publishing." The same month he approached the Academy's publisher, Saillant, from whom he did not receive the expected favorable propositions. He then entrusted the engraving of his twelve plates dealing with watch springs to a Monsieur Benard, who did his work "superbly." Meanwhile Blakey wrote his *l'Art de faire les ressorts à pendules*. He offered his works by public subscription, but, meeting little success, he completely revised his essays, and planned another on the making of elastic bandages for hernias. All these he hoped to publish "in the same format as that of the Academy." They were to serve as a sequel to the *Descriptions* and would be printed on fine paper similar to that used for the others. Shortly afterward, being in Holland on business, he arranged to have his work on watch springs published by Rey at a price of four Dutch florins. He then mentions another study, *Observations sur les pompes à feu, à balancier, et sur les nouvelles machines à feu; avec des remarques sur la situation de la Hollande, et les machines à épuiser les eaux des marais.* This quarto work was in two parts and had the usual plates. This is apparently the treatise of which Morand speaks in the second part of his essay on the exploitation of coal mines, where he mentions on page 201: "l'ouvrage de M. Blakay (*sic*) agréé par l'Académie sur la fabrication des pompes à feu."

## APPENDIX B

### The Neufchâtel Edition

#### Prepared by George B. Watts

Descriptions des arts et métiers faites ou approuvées par messieurs de l'Académie royale des sciences de Paris. Avec figures en taille-douce. Nouvelle édition publiée avec des observations, & augmentée de tout ce qui a été écrit de mieux sur ces matières, en Allemagne, en Angleterre, en Suisse, en Italie. Par J. E. Bertrand. . . Neuchâtel, Imprimerie de la Société typographique, 1771–83.

19 v. plates (part fold.), tables (part fold.). 23 cm.

Volume 1. L'art du meunier; du boulanger; du vermicellier. 1771. Dedicated to the King.
Volume 2. Quatre premières sections sur les fers; et l'art du charbonnier. 1774. Dedicated to Catherine II, Impératrice et Autocratrice de toutes les Russies.
Volume 3. L'art du tanneur, du chamoiseur; du mégissier; du corroyeur; du parcheminier; de l'hongroyeur, du maroquinier; de travailler les cuirs dorés et argentés; du cordonnier; du paumier-raquetier et de la paume. 1774.
Volume 4. L'art du tuilier et du briquetier; l'art de tirer des carrières la pierre d'ardoise, de la fendre et de la tailler; l'art du couvreur; l'art du chaufournier; l'art de faire le papier; l'art du cartonnier; et l'art du cartier. 1776.
Volume 5. Les trois premières sections du traité des pêches et l'histoire des poissons. 1776.
Volume 6. Art du serrurier; art du chandelier; art d'exploiter les mines de charbon de terre. 1776(?)
Volume 7. Art de la draperie; l'art de friser ou ratiner les étoffes de laine; l'art de faire les tapis façon de Turquie; l'art du chapelier; l'art du tonnelier; l'art de convertir le cuivre en laiton; et l'art de l'épinglier. 1777.
Volume 8. L'art de l'indigotier; l'art de la porcelaine; l'art du potier de terre; l'art de faire les pipes; l'art de faire les colles; fabrique de l'amidon; l'art du savonnier; et l'art du relieur. 1777.
Volume 9. Six premières parties de l'art du fabricant d'étoffes de soie. 1779. Dedicated to His Majesty the King of Denmark and Norway.

Volume 10. Deux premières sections de la seconde partie du traité des pêches. 1779.

Volume 11. Troisième section de la seconde partie du traité des pêches. 1779.

Volume 12. L'art du distillateur d'eaux-fortes; l'art du distillateur liquoriste; et l'art du vinaigrier; avec des notes et des additions par M. Struve, Docteur en médecine, et membre de la société physique de Berne. 1780.

Volume 13. L'art de la peinture sur verre et de la vitrerie; et l'art du plombier et fontainier. 1781.

Volume 14. L'art du perruquier; l'art du tailleur, renfermant le tailleur d'habits d'hommes, les culottes de peau, le tailleur de corps de femmes et enfants, la couturière et la marchande de modes; l'art de la lingère; l'art du brodeur; l'art du cirier; l'art du criblier; l'art du coutelier en ouvrages communs; l'art du bourrelier et du sellier; et l'art du mouleur en plâtre. 1780.

Volume 15. Fabrique des ancres; la forge des enclumes; le nouvel art d'adoucir le fer fondu; l'art du faiseur de peignes d'acier pour la fabrique des étoffes de soie; l'art de réduire le fer en fil sous le nom de fil d'archal; l'art de raffiner le sucre; et l'art d'affiner l'argent. 1781.

Volume 16. Trois premières sections de la seconde partie de l'Art d'exploiter les mines de charbon de terre. 1780.

Volume 17. Quatrième section de la seconde partie de l'Art d'exploiter les mines de charbon de terre. 1780.

Volume 18. Table analytique des matières de l'Art d'exploiter les mines de charbon de terre. Un supplément à la notice des opérations tentées en Normandie et en Bourgogne, annoncées dans le troisième article de la dernière partie, et plusieurs additions et corrections. Une nouvelle méthode pour diviser les instruments de mathématique et d'astronomie. La description d'un microscope et de différents micromètres, destinés à mesurer des parties circulaires ou droites, avec la plus grande précision. 1781.

Volume 19. L'art du serrurier, ou essai sur les combinaisons méchaniques, employées particulièrement pour produire l'effet des meilleures serrures ordinaires; l'art de préparer et d'imprimer les étoffes en laines, suivi de l'art de fabriquer les pannes ou peluches, les velours façon d'Utrecht, et les moquettes; l'art du fabricant de velours de coton, précédé d'une dissertation sur la nature, le choix, et la préparation des matières, et suivi d'un traité de la teinture et de l'impression des étoffes de ces mêmes matières; l'art du fabricant d'étoffes en laines; un mémoire concernant l'éducation des troupeaux et la culture des laines, et enfin l'art du tourbier.*

## APPENDIX C

### CONTRIBUTORS TO *Descriptions des Arts et Métiers*

#### Prepared by George B. Watts

Bedos de Celles, Dom François, Benedictine of St. Maur. B. Caux, 1706, d. Nov. 25, 1779. Entered order of Benedictines in Toulouse in 1726. Correspondent of the Royal Academy of Sciences, member of Academy of Sciences of Bordeaux. Several remarkable organs have been attributed to him, especially that of the Cathedral of Bordeaux. His *L'art du facteur d'orgues* has been called "the most famous treatise on organ making ever written." Shared in preparation of *Art du relieur-doreur de livres*. Author of *Gnomonique ou*

* It is noteworthy that several items of the Neufchâtel version do not appear in the Paris original. For example, volume 15 contains *l'Art du mouleur en plâtre* by M. Fiquet: volume 15 has the *Nouvelle méthode d'affiner l'argent*, a translation from the German of J. H. G. von Justi, *Die Kunst das Silber zu affinieren*: volume 19 has Botterman's *Supplément à l'art du serrurier*, and Roland de la Platière's *l'art du tourbier*. Following this last item there is a letter from Amiens on August 20, 1782, in which Roland de la Platière informs the publishers that his treatise had been submitted to the examiners of the Royal Academy of Sciences, and that they had read it, made corrections, and added notes. Their approval not being forthcoming, the author, although "convinced of their good intentions," was persuaded that "the 'Whys?' would never end," and accordingly he had demanded the return of his study "in a very decided manner." Demachy's *Art du vinaigrier* is found in volume 12.

*art de tracer les cadrans solaires*, and *Examen du nouvel orgue construit à Saint-Martin de Tours*, printed in *Mercure de France*, January, 1762.

Bouchu, Étienne-J. B. Langres, May 23, 1714, d. Arc, Sept. 16, 1770. Member of the Academy of Dijon, and correspondent of the Royal Academy of Sciences. Master of the forges at Veux-Saules, near Châteauvilain. Author of article *Forges* in *Encyclopédie*. Quérard states that he wrote all the articles on iron in *Encyclopédie*.

Chapman, Fredrik Henrik. Swedish engineer of English origin. B. Goteborg, Sept. 9, 1721, d. 1808. Worked for two years in the shipyards of England, then studied science of shipbuilding in Sweden, France, England, and Holland. In 1757 he was assigned task of preparing models for a Swedish flotilla for the defense of the coast of Finland. Named chief of naval construction in 1764. Ennobled in 1772. Commissioned rear-admiral in 1781, vice-admiral in 1791. Directed construction of many vessels of the line and many frigates, using the parabolic method invented by him, and which was adopted by English shipbuilders. Author of *Architectura navalis mercatoria*, 1768; *De la voilure des vaisseaux de ligne*, 1791, Eng. tr. 1794; *Essai sur la dimension et les formes à donner aux vaisseaux de ligne et aux frégates*, 1804; and many memoirs on naval matters in the Acts of the Academy of Sciences of Stockholm.

Chaulnes, Michel-Ferdinand d'Albert d'Ailly, duc de. B. 1714, d. 1769. With his wife Anne-Joseph Bonnier he devoted himself to the study of physical and natural sciences. Named honorary member of Royal Academy of Sciences in 1743. Left several memoirs in the collection of the Academy and in *Le Journal de Physique*.

Courtivron, Gaspard Le Compasseur de Créquy-Montfort, marquis de. B. château of Courtivron, 1715, d. 1785. Member of Royal Academy of Sciences from 1744. He first embraced the military career and was commissioned colonel. Author of *Traité de l'optique, où l'on donne la théorie de la lumière dans le système Newtonien*, 1752, and many memoirs in the collection of the Academy on varied subjects, such as: physics, mathematics, sicknesses of cattle, and metallurgy. Of him the *Encyclopédie* says: "well known in the republic of letters through many memoirs on optics and physics. . . His enlightened patriotism appears especially in the memoir on the cattle sickness which broke out . . . in Is-sur-Thil, and the remedies which he proposed for it." He contributed the section *Des couvertures en lave* in *Art du Couvreur*.

Demachy, Jacques-François. B. Paris, Aug. 30, 1728, d. July 7, 1803. Student of Collège de Beauvais. Wrote poetry, which was published in *Almanach des muses* and *Mercure de France*. Obtained a position in the laboratory of the Hôtel-Dieu, and for twenty-five years was professor of medical matters. Given the post of chief pharmacist of the military hospital of St.-Denis, and later the directorship of the central pharmacy of the civil hospitals. Royal censor. Member of the Royal Academy of Sciences and many other bodies. Author of many works on chemistry and several manuscript comedies of second order. Among his writings are: *Art du vinaigrier*, *Nouveaux dialogues des morts*, *Dissertations chimiques de Pott* (tr. from German and Latin), *Économie rustique*, *Éléments de chimie* (tr. from Latin), *Examen chimique des eaux de Passy*, *Examen des eaux minérales de Verberie*, *Instituts de chimie*, 2 vol., *Manuel du pharmacien*, 2 vol., and *Procédés chimiques rangés méthodiquement et définis*, etc.

Duhamel du Monceau, Henri-Louis. For his life and career, see p. 11. Among his many works are: *Éléments d'agriculture*, *École d'agriculture*, *Éléments d'architecture navale*, *De l'exploitation des bois*, *Histoire d'un insecte qui dévore les grains de l'Angoumois*, *Moyens de conserver la santé aux équipages des vaisseaux*, etc., *La physique des arbres*, *Des semis et plantations des arbres, et de leur culture*, *Traité de la culture des terres, suivant les principes de Tull*, 6 v., *Traité de la fabrique, des manoeuvres pour les vaisseaux, ou l'art de la corderie perfectionné*, *Traité de la garance, et de sa culture*, *Traité des arbres et arbustes qui se cultivent en France en pleine terre*, 2 v., *Traité des arbres fruitiers*, etc., *Traité des bois, et des différentes manières de les semer, planter, cultiver, exploiter, et conserver*, 2 v., *Traité sur la nature et sur la culture de la vigne*, 2 v., *Du transport, de la conservation et de la force des bois*, and a very long list of memoirs in the collection of the Academy. The *Encyclopédie* drew largely from his description of making pipes for its article *Pipes* in the *Supplément*.

Fougeroux de Bondaroy, Auguste Denis. B. Paris, 1732, nephew of Duhamel du Monceau, d. 1789. Enjoyed a certain fortune which gave him independence so that he could devote his life to the study of natural sciences. His labors produced important perfections in rural economy and new methods in the arts and handicrafts of his day. He was the author of *Recherches sur les ruines d'Herculanum, etc., Observations faites sur les côtes de Normandie, Mémoire sur la formation des os*, and a large number of memoirs in the collection of the Academy. With Thenin and Teissier he prepared the section on agriculture for *Encyclopédie*, and had assumed responsibility for the articles on woods and forests for the Panckoucke edition, dying before completing the task, and leaving many notes.

Fourcroy de Ramecourt, Charles-René. B. Paris, Jan. 19, 1715, d. Jan. 12, 1791. The son of a Parisian lawyer, he was trained for the bar. After practicing law until the age of twenty-five he abandoned that profession for a military career, entering the corps of engineers in 1736. Took part in all the campaigns of the war of 1740, became *maréchal de camp*, and director general of the royal engineering corps. During periods of peace he busied himself with research and experiments in physics, natural history, and technology. Admitted to Royal Academy of Sciences in 1784. The microscopic observations in Senac's *Traité du coeur* are said to have been almost entirely by him. He supplied many of the observations for Duhamel's *Traité des pesches*, and materials for Lalande's study of the tides. He was the author of *Mémoires sur la fortification perpendiculaire, Plan de communication entre l'Escaut, la Sambre, l'Oise, la Meuse, la Moselle et le Rhin, etc., Observations sur les marées à la côte de Flandre*, and *Observations sur une illusion d'optique*.

Galon, —, colonel of infantry, royal engineer at Ghent, and chief engineer of Le Havre, correspondent of the Royal Academy of Sciences, d. 1775.

Garsault, François-Alexandre. B. 1691(?), d. 1778. A zealous student, he devoted his life to varied researches, especially in veterinary medicine, horsemanship, mechanics, natural history, literature, and the arts. Appointed captain of the stud farms of France. Member of the Royal Academy of Sciences. A skilled artist, he executed many of the engravings for his works. His *Anatomie générale du cheval* (tr. from English), with plates drawn and engraved by Garsault is said to be the first complete treatise on the anatomy of the horse published in France. Among his works are: *Le guide du cavalier, Éléments de géographie historique, à l'usage des lycées et des collèges, Faits des causes célèbres et intéressantes, etc., Guide du cavalier, Traité des voitures, Description abrégée de 719 plantes et 154 animaux, Le nouveau parfait maréchal*, and *Figures des plantes et animaux d'usage en médecine*.

Hellot, Jean. B. Nov. 20, 1685 in Paris, d. Feb. 15, 1766. Famous chemist, member of the Royal Society of London and the Royal Academy of Sciences. Author of *Art de la teinture des laines et des étoffes de laine, etc., De la fonte des mines et des fonderies* (tr. from German), and many memoirs in the collection of the Academy of Sciences.

Hulot, —. B. about 1715, d. in Paris in 1781. Said to have been one of the most skillful mechanics and turners of his time. Studied mathematics and statistics, as well as practical chemistry, alloys, dyeing of wood, bone, and ivory, and the tempering of steel. He developed several ingenious machines, such as lathes for guilloche work, and platforms for the drive wheels of clocks. For more precision in clock making, he constructed in bronze a set of dividers of two meters in diameter.

Jars, Gabriel. B. in Lyons, Jan. 26, 1732, d. in Clermont, Aug. 20, 1769. Member of Royal Academy of Sciences, the Society of Arts of London, and the Academy of Lyon. After finishing his studies he was summoned by his father to assist him in the exploitation of the mines of Sainbel and Chessy. From 1757 to 1766 he visited the mines of Saxony, Austria, Bohemia, Styria, England, the Harz, Norway, and Sweden. From these travels he brought back the data for several memoirs, and important improvements which he introduced into the management of the French mines. These travels are described in his *Voyages métallurgiques, ou recherches et observations sur les mines et forges de fer, la fabrication d'acier, celle du fer-blanc, et plusieurs mines de charbon de terre, etc.* Quérard says that at the time Jars began his travels the French were far behind the other countries of Europe in the science of mineralogy and metallurgy, and that he "rendered a veritable service to his country in enabling it to know better two sciences of the greatest interest for its industry."

La Gardette, Abbé Claude-Mathieu de. Architect of the medical school of Montpellier, former student of the school of fine arts of Rome, and member of the Society of sciences, belles-lettres and arts of Paris. Author of *Essai sur la restauration des piliers du dôme du Panthéon français, Nouvelles règles pour la pratique du dessin et du lavis de l'architecture civile et militaire*, and *Les ruines de Paestum ou de Posidonia, ancienne et moderne ville de la Grande-Grèce, mesurées et dessinées sur les lieux*.

Lalande, Joseph-Jérôme Le Français de. One of the most distinguished and perhaps best known of the eighteenth-century French astronomers. B. July 11, 1732 at Bourg en Bresse, d. in Paris, April 4, 1807. He went to Paris to study law, but as a result of a visit to the Observatory he decided to follow the courses in astronomy of Delisle and Le Monnier at the Collège de France. In order to attach him definitely to the study of astronomy Le Monnier sent him in 1751 on a mission to Berlin to determine the parallax of the moon. After his return he spent some time in Bourg where his parents wished him to practice law, but in 1753 he returned to Paris. He was admitted to the Royal Academy of Sciences and began to submit memoirs of which he produced more than one hundred. In 1760 he took Delisle's place as professor of astronomy at the Collège de France. He served as director of the Observatory until his death. He wrote many articles for the *Journal des Savants*, the *Journal de Physique*, the *Magazin encyclopédique*, and the memoirs of various academies. He served as editor of *Connaissance des temps* and *Journal des Savants*. As editor he published several new editions of works on mathematics, navigation, and astronomy, including Fontenelle's *Entretiens sur la pluralité des mondes*. He was the author of all the articles on astronomy in the supplement to *Encyclopédie*. Member of the Royal Academy of Sciences, the Marine Academy at Brest, and of the Academies of London, Berlin, Saint Petersburg, Stockholm, Copenhagen, and Boulogne. Among his published works are *Voyage d'un Français en Italie*, 8 v., *Exposition du calcul astronomique, Astronomie, Astronomie des dames, Tables astronomiques, Abrégé de navigation, Histoire céleste française, Bibliographie astronomique*, and *Tables de la lune*. Of him it has been said: "Lalande wrote too much for his work not often to leave something to be desired, but he did much useful work and rendered real services to science, occupying himself especially with the practical side."

Le Monnier, Pierre-Charles. B. Paris, Nov. 23, 1715, d. in Héric, May 31, 1799. At the age of sixteen he observed the opposition of Saturn. He was received into the Royal Academy of Sciences at the age of twenty-one, having presented to it in 1735 a new lunar map. He was named to accompany P. L. Maupertuis and Alexis Clairault on their geodetical expedition to Lapland. Shortly after his return he read before the Academy a memoir in which he explained the advantages of J. Flamsteed's mode of determining right ascensions. His recommendations of English methods and instruments contributed much to the reform of French practical astronomy. In 1741 he introduced the use of the transit-instrument at the Paris Observatory. Went to England in 1748 and, with the Earl of Morton and James Short, he observed the annular eclipse in Scotland. He was able to measure the diameter of the moon against the disk of the sun. He made important series of lunar observations, researches in terrestrial magnetism, and determined the places of many stars. In his lectures at the Collège de France he first publicly expounded the analytical theory of gravitation. First doctor ordinary of Louis XV. Royal professor of botany. Member of the Royal Academy of Sciences, the Royal Society of London, and the Academy of Berlin. Contributed several articles for *Encyclopédie*. Author of *Astronomie nautique lunaire, etc., Essai sur les marées, Exposition des moyens les plus faciles de résoudre plusieurs questions dans l'art de la navigation, etc., Histoire céleste, Les lois du magnétisme, etc.*, 2 v., *Nouveau zodiaque, réduit à l'année 1755, Observations sur la lune, du soleil, et des étoiles fixes, etc.*, and *Théorie des comètes*.

Le Vieil, Pierre. B. Paris, 1708, d. Paris, Feb. 23, 1772. His father was a well-known glass painter, commissioned by Mansard to execute the glass friezes of the chapel of Versailles and the dome of the Invalides. Pierre showed great promise at the Collège de St.-Barbi and the Collège de la Marche. At seventeen years he became a postulant in the order of St. Benoît, but, feeling that it was his duty to return home to assist his parents, he left the order "to the great regret of his superiors." In 1734 he restored with great success the glass of the ossuary of St. Étienne du Mont. He also did restorations in the glass of Notre Dame, the church of St. Victor, the Hôtel Dieu, the Carmes (Place Maubert), and several colleges of the university. He was the author of *Essai sur la peinture en mosaïque* and a Christian tragedy, *Saint Romain, martyr*, in three acts in prose, written for the Ursulines at Crespi.

Lucotte, J. R. Architect of Paris, author of *Le Vignole moderne, ou traité élémentaire d'architecture*, in three parts.

Macquer, Pierre-Joseph. B. Paris, October 9, 1718, d. Paris, Feb. 15, 1784. Doctor of medicine in 1742. Especially interested in chemistry. Louis XV charged him with the direction of the Sevres porcelain factory. Academy of Sciences in 1745. Member of Academy of Turin. Named royal censor and professor of chemistry of the Jardin du Roi. Author of *Dictionnaire de chimie*, 2 v., *Éléments de chimie pratique*, 2 v., *Éléments de chimie théorique*, 2 v., *Formulae medicamentorum magistralium*, *Manuel du naturaliste*, *Pharmacopoea parisiensis*, and *Plan d'un cours de chimie expérimentale et raisonnée*. With Baumé he contributed articles for the *Journal des Savants*.

Malouin, Paul-Jacques. B. Caen, 1701, d. Paris, Jan. 3, 1788. He was sent to Paris for law studies but became interested in medicine and received his doctor's degree. Soon won a wide reputation. Named professor at the Collège de France, doctor ordinary of the queen, and professor of chemistry in the Jardin du Roi. Member of the Royal Academy of Sciences and Royal Society of London. He attached a high importance to preventive medicine and imposed upon himself a severe regimen which procured for him a vigorous old age. He was the author of many articles in *Encyclopédie* dealing with chemistry and signed "M." In the supplement to *Encyclopédie* several articles are based on his *Art du vermicelier*. Among his published works are: *Chimie médicinale, contenant la manière de préparer les remèdes les plus usités*, 2 v., *Traité de chimie, contenant la manière de préparer les remèdes qui sont les plus en usage dans la pratique de la médecine*, *Traité des chances*, and *Traité sur les rentes viagères*.

Morand, Jean François Clément. B. Paris, 1726, d. Paris, Aug. 13, 1784. Doctor of medicine in 1750 and professor of anatomy at Collège de France. Member of Royal Academy of Sciences and of the Academies of Stockholm, Harlem, and Brussels, and of various learned societies of Madrid, Florence, Berne, Liége, and the Royal Society of London. Secretary of the Royal Society of Surgery. Contributed materials for articles in *Encyclopédie* and several memoirs in the collections of the Academy of Sciences. Author of *Mémoires sur la nature, les effets et avantages du feu de charbon de terre, etc.*, *Mémoire sur la qualité dangereuse de l'émétique qui se prépare chez les apothicaires de Lyon*, *Recherches anatomiques sur les rats*, *Question de médecine sur les hermaphrodites*, and many *Lettres* on various remedies and sicknesses. He prepared himself for his study of coal mining by visiting the coal mines of Liége, Newcastle, and Manchester.

Nollet, Jean-Antoine, Abbé. B. Pimbré, Nov. 19, 1700, son of poor farmers, d. Paris, April 25, 1770. Educated at colleges of Clermont and Beauvais. Sent to Paris for studies in philosophy. Licensed in theology by the faculty of Paris. Received permission to be excused from preaching and devoted himself to the study of physics. Soon became distinguished for the number and quality of his experiments in electricity, performed in Réaumur's laboratory. In 1734 he travelled in England with Dufay, Duhamel, and Jussieu. Travelled in Holland, returning to Paris to resume his course in experimental physics. Member of the Royal Academy of Sciences and the Royal Society. Professor of physics to the Dauphin. Went twice to Italy to study arts and agriculture. In addition to some twenty memoirs in the Academy's collection, he was the author of several works, the majority of which dealt with the study of physics. Among them are: *Leçons de physique expérimentale*, 6 v., (frequently reprinted). *Lettres sur l'éléctricité* (numbers 2–7 are addressed to Benjamin Franklin), *Recherches sur les causes particulières des phénomènes éléctriques*, and *Art des expériences, etc.*, 3 v.

Paulet, Jean. Son of a silk manufacturer of Nîmes. Of him Michaud says: "After having learned the trade he made a study of the theory and won the approbation of the Academy for his description of the trade."

Perret, Jean-Jacques. B. Béziers, July 30, 1730, d. Paris, April 2, 1784. Son of a poor cutler, he left Béziers at the age of twelve to make his tour of France. Admitted into one of the largest establishments in Paris, he joined to his great skill a profound study of the art. Responsible for great progress in the art of making surgical instruments. Became one of the most distinguished anatomists of his day. Became provost of the cutlers of Paris and the head of an important cutlery house. Among his important developments were an instrument designed to make sections of the transparent cornea in cataract operations and a composition for polishing steel. Correspondent of the academy of Béziers and honorary associate of the society of arts of Geneva. Author of *Mémoire sur l'acier, dans lequel on traite des différentes qualités de ce métal; de la forge, du bon emploi et de la trempe*, and *Pogonotomie, ou l'art d'apprendre à se raser soi-même, etc.*

Perronet, Jean Rodolphe. B. Suresnes, 1708, d. Feb. 27, 1794. Engineer of highways and bridges, member of the Royal Academy of Architecture, Academy of Stockholm, and Royal Society of London. Author of several published works on the construction of bridges, stone arches, and the canalization to Paris of the waters of the Yvette and the Bievre. Contributed several memoirs to the collections of the Academy of Sciences, and the article, *Pompes à feu* in *Encyclopédie*. Inspector-general of the French salt mines.

Réaumur, René-Antoine Ferchault de. For his life and career, see pp. 8–9. Among his important publications are: *l'Art de convertir le fer forgé en acier, et l'art d'adoucir le fer fondu, ou de faire des ouvrages de fer fondu aussi finis que de fer forgé, Art de faire éclore et d'élever en toute saison des oiseaux domestiques, de toutes espèces, soit par le moyen de la chaleur du fumier, soit par le moyen du feu ordinaire, Mémoires pour servir à l'histoire des insectes, Mémoires sur les cabinets d'histoire naturelle, Mémoires sur les oiseaux, Avis pour donner du secours à ceux que l'on croit noyés.* Of the six volume work on insects Quérard says: "Of all the works to appear in the XVIIIth century, this is the one which contributed the most to natural history."

Roland de la Platière, Jean-Marie. B. 1732 in Villefranche, d. by suicide near Rouen, Nov. 10, 1793. Family distinguished in the law but in straightened circumstances. He left home intending to seek fortune abroad, but illness forced him to abandon project. After working as clerk he joined a relative who was inspector of manufactures, and he soon rose to position of inspector-general of the manufactures of Picardy. In 1781 he married Manon Jeanne Phlipon, the famous Madame Roland. About 1785 they moved to Lyons. A correspondence sprang up with Brissot and other friends of the Revolution in Paris, and in 1791 the Rolands settled there. Her salon soon became the meeting place of several leaders of the popular movement. He joined the Jacobin Club. On March 23, 1792 he became minister of the interior. As minister of the crown he "exhibited a bourgeois brusqueness of manner and a remarkable combination of political prejudice and administrative ability." Soon after reading a letter to the king in full council in which there were "many and terrible truths as to royal refusal to sanction decrees, and as to the king's position in the state," Roland was dismissed. He then read his letter to the Assembly. It was printed and widely circulated, becoming the manifesto of dissatisfaction. Roland was recalled to power after the insurrection of August 10, but he became dismayed at the progress of the Revolution. In the trial of the king he demanded, with the Girondists, that sentence should be pronounced by a vote of the whole people, not simply by the Convention. He resigned his office January 23, 1793, two days after the execution of the king. The Rolands remained in Paris, and on June 1 Madame Roland was imprisoned in the Abbaye. He escaped to Rouen. When he heard of his wife's execution on November 8, 1793, he committed suicide by falling on his swordstick. Among his published works are: *Lettres écrites de Suisse, d'Italie, de Sicile et de Malte, Le financier patriote, etc., Dictionnaire des manufactures et des arts qui en dépendent*, 4 v., (this is his contribution to the Panckoucke edition of *Encyclopédie*), *Aux corps administratifs, Mémoire sur l'éducation des troupeaux et la culture des laines*, and a great many opuscules, reports, and minutes on political matters.

Romme, Nicolas Charles. B. Riom, about 1744, d. Rochefort, June, 1805. Studied in Paris where he became intimate friend of Lalande who procured for him the post of royal professor of mathematics and navigation at the naval school of Rochefort. Correspondent of Royal Academy of Sciences and later first class of the Institut. He left several published works, among which are: *Mémoire où l'on propose une nouvelle méthode pour déterminer les longitudes en mer, L'art de la marine, Dictionnaire de la marine française, Dictionnaire de la marine anglaise, Tableau des vents, des marées, et des courants*, and *Science de l'homme*

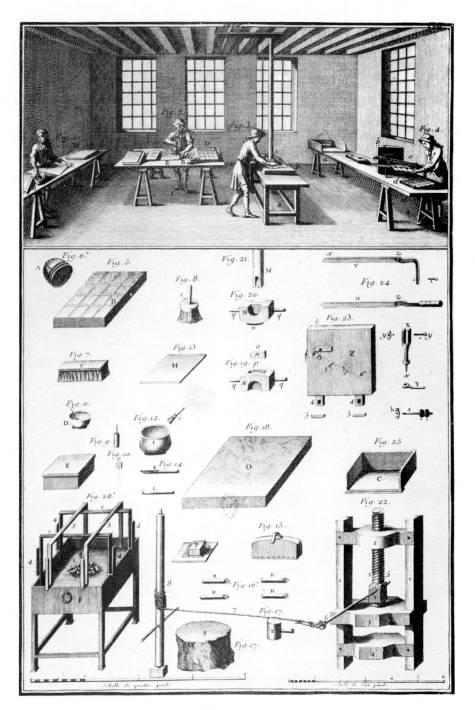

A typical illustration from a volume of the *Descriptions* — this one from Duhamel
du Monceau's *Art du cartier*.

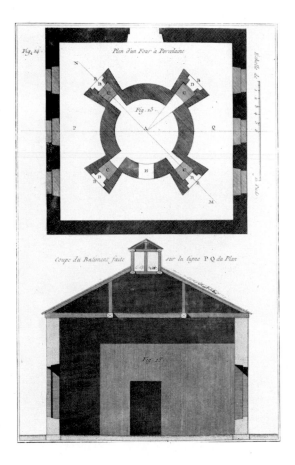
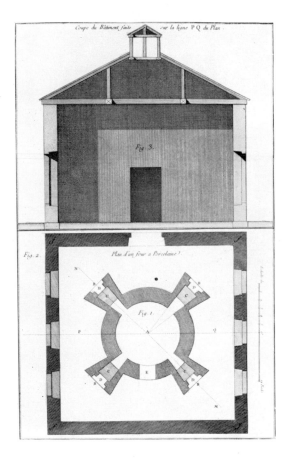

EVIDENCE OF PLAGIARISM

At the left, a plate from the Supplement to the *Encyclopedie* (1777), and, at the right, one from Comte de Milly's
*Art de la Porcelaine* (1771).

*de mer.* Of him it has been said: "one of the savants who contributed the most to the progress of navigation in the eighteenth century."

Roubu, Jacques André. B. Paris, 1739, d. Paris, 1791. Received from his father, a master cabinet-maker, a very sound education. Studied mathematics, mechanics, and design. After his *Art du menuisier* had been accepted by the Academy, it requested for him the mastership. He "offers the phenomenon, rarer in France than in the rest of Europe of a workman who was distinguished in his state and who never thought of giving it up for a higher profession."

Saint-Aubin, Charles Germain de. B. Paris, 1721, d. Paris, March 17, 1786. One of fourteen children of Gabriel Germain de Saint-Aubin, engraver by appointment to the king, and oldest of four sons who became engravers. His father taught him design which he employed especially in embroidery patterns. He received a commission as royal designer for modern costumes. Remembered for several series of etchings "done with as much wit as originality." Among these are his *Essais de papillonneries humaines* (representing butterflies playing human roles), *Mes petits bouquets*, and *Les Fleurettes*.

Thy, Nicolas Christiern de, Comte de Milly. B. June 18, 1728 of an ancient and illustrious family of Beaujolais, died in Chaillot, Sept. 17, 1784. Entered military service at an early age and became commanding colonel in the Dragoons, chevalier of St. Louis, and first honorary lieutenant of the Swiss Guards of Monsieur, Comte de Provence (later Louis XVIII). After the battle of Minden, Thy, disgusted with the French service, entered the forces of Charles Eugene, Duke of Württemberg. He was named adjutant general, chamberlain, and chevalier of the Red Eagle. After declaration of peace he returned to France and devoted himself to the study of sciences, especially chemistry and physics. In his laboratory of Chaillot he analysed and tried many mysterious remedies, as a result of which he is believed to have died poisoned. Member of the academies of sciences of Harlem, Madrid, Lyons, and Dijon, and an associate of the Royal Academy of Sciences. Author of *Anti-Siphilytique, ou la santé publique*, *Mémoire sur la manière d'essuyer les murs nouvellement faits*, and many memoirs in the Academy's collection and in the *Journal de Physique*. The article "porcelaine" in the supplement to *Encyclopédie* was "borrowed" from his *L'art de la Porcelaine.**

* Most of the data of Appendix C have been taken from Quérard, *La France Littéraire, Grande Encyclopédie*, Michaud, *Biographie Universelle*, and *Nouvelle Biographie Générale*, etc. (Firmin Didot).